Space
to Imagine

Study Creative Writing at Bath Spa

The Creative Writing Centre at Bath Spa University has been helping people get published for over three decades. We are now accepting applications for Autumn 2012 entry onto the following programmes of study:

MA Creative Writing

MA Writing for Young People

MA Scriptwriting

MA Travel & Nature Writing

PhD Creative Writing

www.bathspa.ac.uk/schools/humanities-and-cultural-industries/creative-writing

GRANTA

12 Addison Avenue, London W11 4QR

email editorial@granta.com

To subscribe go to www.granta.com

Or call 845-267-3031 (toll-free 866-438-6150) in the United States, 020 8955 7011 in the United Kingdom

ISSUE 118: WINTER 2012

This selection copyright © 2012 Granta Publications

In the United States, *Granta* is published in association with Grove/Atlantic Inc., 841 Broadway, 4th Floor, New York, NY 10003, and distributed by PGW. All editorial queries should be addressed to the London office.

Granta USPS 000-508 is published four times per year (February, May, August and November) by *Granta*, 12 Addison Avenue, London W11 4QR, United Kingdom, at the annual subscription rate of £34.95 and $45.99.

Airfreight and mailing in the USA by Agent named Air Business, c/o Worldnet Shipping USA Inc., 149–35 177th Street, Jamaica, New York, NY 11434. Periodicals postage paid at Jamaica, NY 11431.

US POSTMASTER: Send address changes to *Granta*, PO Box 359, Congers, NY 10920-0359.

Granta is printed and bound in Italy by Legoprint. This magazine is printed on paper that fulfils the criteria for 'Paper for permanent document' according to ISO 9706 and the American Library Standard ANSI/NIZO Z39.48-1992 and has been certified by the Forest Stewardship Council (FSC). *Granta* is indexed in the American Humanities Index.

ISBN 978-1-905881-55-0

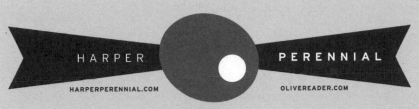

NEW FROM
HARPER PERENNIAL

Waterline
a novel by Ross Raisin

The Ruins of Us
a novel by Keija Parssinen

"Raisin confirms himself as an exciting talent, a unique, gifted, and generous voice."
—David Vann,
Financial Times

"Arresting... [Parssinen's] evocative petrol universe of wealth, privilege, and intrigue is unforgettable. Powerful storytelling that is refreshing and entertaining."
—Anthony Swofford,
author of *Jarhead*

The Reconstructionist
a novel by Nick Arvin

Further Interpretations of Real-Life Events
Stories by Kevin Moffett

A stunning new novel of secrets and survival from an acclaimed literary voice.

"Stops the traffic in more ways than one."
—*Financial Times*

"Kevin Moffett's stories are stealth heartbreakers, as well as wonders of sly detail and perfect tone. He's writing some of the best short fiction around."
—Sam Lipsyte

Beyond Ballets Russes

Celebrating the legacy of Diaghilev's legendary company

"Ballet is powerful, in beauty and horror, as this outstanding programme demonstrates"

The Daily Telegraph

ENGLISH NATIONA BALLE

22 March – 1 April
London Coliseum
Tickets £10 - £67

www.ballet.org.uk

Supported by
ARTS COUNCIL ENGLAND

CONTENTS

7 **The Road to Damascus**
Claire Messud

29 **Poem**
Adrienne Rich

31 **Thirty Girls**
Susan Minot

51 **City Boy**
Judy Chicurel

69 **Summer**
Jacob Newberry

87 **The Interrogation**
Vanessa Manko

103 **Poem**
Ishion Hutchinson

105 **America**
Chinelo Okparanta

128 **The Island**
Stacy Kranitz

137 **The Provincials**
Daniel Alarcón

173 **The Beginner's Goodbye**
Anne Tyler

192 **Poem**
Paula Bohince

193 **Anecdotes**
Ann Beattie

208 **Poem**
Sophie Cabot Black

209 **Bonfire**
David Long

219 **In Sight of the Lake**
Alice Munro

235 **The End?**
John Barth

241 **War Dogs**
Aleksandar Hemon

254 Notes on contributors

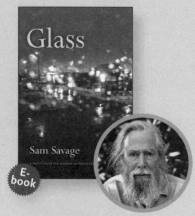
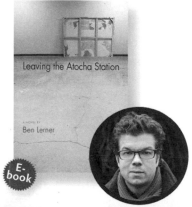

THE ROAD TO DAMASCUS

Claire Messud

I

I went to Beirut in June of 2010 because my father was dying.
This sentence, palpably illogical – my father was not dying in
Beirut – is nonetheless true.

When my father was in hospital in 2008, after nearly dying
from a perforated ulcer, then from MRSA, the doctors said to him,
categorically, 'You drink, you die.' We all heard them. We talked about
it. And for almost two years, he did not drink, and he didn't die.

And then, early in 2010, in remission from a cancer diagnosed a
year before that, he started drinking again. I don't know whether he
died because he drank; or whether he drank because he was sure he
was going to die; or because he was afraid to die and wanted to forget
about it; or because he just wanted, by then, to die. It is strange to
understand that all of these can be true at once. Suffice it to say: he
drank; he died.

In late April of 2010, my father had a stroke. They realized, once he
was in hospital, that after a respite of ten months his oesophageal
cancer was back in force. His throat was fully dammed: there was not
even room in his gullet for his spit to slip down to his stomach. The
oncologist – a bluff fellow of the old school, eminently clubbable,
who prided himself on his frankness and resembled British generals
in black-and-white war films, with his bow tie and his tidy white
moustache – confided, oddly jauntily, in the hallway outside my
father's room, 'Within six to eight weeks he'll be in trouble.'

In between the oncologist's first prognosis in the corridor of the hospital and my father's last breath, there was a Bergsonian eternity, moment upon moment upon moment of Being. My father was always intolerant of small talk and banality: he very much wanted time to *mean*. In this sense, those last three months of his life were very much his time. But inevitably, too, there was stupid time, interspersed between significant time – time that wouldn't necessarily, in ordinary circumstances, have been considered stupid, but which, in the context of death, became strangely preposterous. Watching television of course becomes impossible in a crisis. But even the matter of living my own life became largely absurd to me: teaching classes, participating in panel discussions, attending readings – ridiculous. Perhaps ironically, the daily household tasks, when rarely I was at home with my family, seemed immensely precious: making breakfast, folding the clothes, the small connections to the ordinary, a place where we wanted the children at all costs to remain.

Some months before, I had committed to going to teach in Beirut for a fortnight in the second half of June. When the oncologist first gave my father six to eight weeks, it was the beginning of May. Six weeks would coincide almost exactly with my departure for Beirut; eight weeks with my return. I didn't know what to do, whether to cancel the trip straight away. Two years before, when my father was so ill, I had cancelled everything, stopped my life altogether. Afterwards, I came closer to jumping off a bridge than ever before. This time, with this knowledge, it didn't seem a good idea simply to withdraw.

'Just wait and see,' said my husband, my sister, the doctors. 'Just wait and see.'

For some weeks, my father seemed still to be getting better. He had physical rehab sessions and his walking improved. He ate well (they had put in a stent, a wire mesh, as I understood it, not unlike one you might use in gardening, to keep his oesophagus open), although he complained of the soft food: puréed meat in gravy, mashed potatoes, puréed carrots. We brought him little things he liked to eat and could manage: chocolate truffles, olives, caviar.

He was on enormous doses of painkillers, and when they were not working well he complained of great pain. But in the time after they kicked in and before he slept, or after he slept, he was utterly himself. We talked about things we could never have discussed before: whether he believed in God and believed in an afterlife; whether he was afraid to die; whether he was happy with his life. We pushed his wheelchair around the lovely gardens of the nursing home, pausing by the stone Buddha, counting rabbits, keeping track of the blooming and wilting of flowers, watching the planes fly overhead. We kept an eye out for the jewelled hummingbirds that hovered over the roses and lilies; we monitored the slow disintegration of the fairy village my children had built out of sticks and leaves in a flower bed one drizzling Saturday.

But as the weeks went by and my time to leave approached, my father was clearly suffering more. By the end of May, they had stopped his rehabilitation. The stretches when he was awake and not in pain grew shorter; the pain, when it was present, grew more intense. One of the nurses explained that it was as if a digger were scooping away at his insides: an internal excavation.

And still I clung to the prospect of Beirut. I was to teach at the American University there, a trip organized by the International Writing Program at Iowa in conjunction with AUB, with assistance from the State Department. It was the pilot programme for a possible regular summer teaching course; only two of us were going, a poet and myself, a fiction writer. In those weeks, as I waited for the details of the trip, I had in my mind the State Department-sponsored visit I'd made to Istanbul several years before – a week of classes and meetings with writers and university professors and students, a trip that offered me the promise of Turkish culture like a glorious flower unfolding, mysterious and immense and amazing. The teeming enormity that is Istanbul and the intensity of my encounters had imparted to that visit a particular aura of necessity. It had seemed important to go to Istanbul; it had seemed important *for me* to go to Istanbul; it had seemed important for me to go *at that time* to Istanbul.

Needless to say, Istanbul was also bound up with my father. Istanbul was the first city my father had consciously fallen in love with, as a French boy of ten, arriving at its mouth by boat with his family in the middle of the Second World War. My grandfather, who was sentimental, described it as a *coup de foudre* for his child. My father, who was, if not less sentimental, considerably more reserved, conceded that he had wanted from the first to go back there.

My grandfather was a consular attaché in the French Navy, at that point under orders from Vichy, and so my young father and his younger sister were boarded outside the city at the residence of the Sisters of Our Lady of Sion in Therapia, where they spent the forty days that their parents remained in Istanbul. My grandparents, briefly childless, inhabited a furnished flat overlooking the Bosphorus and engaged in minor derring-do, befriending *sub rosa* the English envoy to Turkey, a man named Ellerington, who would resurface later in the war in Algiers when they were finally all officially on the same side. My father and aunt were photographed, meanwhile, tiny and lost in the overgrown gardens of the *pensionnat* in Therapia, where few children remained because it was summertime.

Over those weeks, my father and aunt learned to swim in the Bosphorus. The children were tied under the armpits with ropes and dropped into the water by a near-nun (it would seem that the Sisters of Sion were complicatedly nunnish but not fully nuns) in a near-habit who then paraded up and down the jetty holding on to this lead. In this way the children, ostensibly undrownable, swam several lengths without being drawn out into the Strait by the swift current to perish at sea. I am not sure whether the swimming mistress held the rope of one child at a time, or of several children at once, like a dog-walker in Central Park.

More than half a century later, my father remembered the beauty of the light on the Bosphorus, the precise yet glaucous outlines of the buildings in Sultanahmet in the early day. He had held that beauty in his mind's eye, in palimpsest – the overlaid and changing memory of all his visits to the city. He first returned to Istanbul as a teenager, for a summer, as soon as he was able to travel alone, and had his wallet and passport stolen before ever he arrived at the port – a vanishing which seemed somehow symbolic: to be searching, in the maze of a city, for something essential and irretrievable, as for some impossible belonging.

Much later, he learned Turkish and embarked upon a PhD at Harvard on Turkish political parties. He and my mother passed through Istanbul on their way to Ankara, where they lived for six months in the late 1950s in order for him to pursue his research. She, not yet thirty, fresh from Toronto, whose limited travel experience had been entirely in Western Europe, wrote home detailed and emotional letters to her parents, describing what it was like for a young Canadian woman in Ankara in 1959: her indignation when she witnessed a bus driver deliberately running over a dog; the thrill of collecting shards of ancient pottery at a friend's archaeological dig; her alternating frustration and amusement at the daily struggles to communicate with the housekeeper. She approved of the food (I have a battered paperback cookbook of hers, published in Ankara in 1958, in the front of which she has scrawled her own recipes for tabouleh and hummus), although not as much as my father, who would all his life love this cuisine best of any. He, meanwhile, filled a briefcase with notes in his spiky scrawl, in French and English and Turkish, a briefcase that moulders still in the basement of my parents' house in Canada and which some day soon I will have to find the courage to throw away.

My father abandoned the PhD – my mother did not ultimately care for life in Ankara; and besides, my father felt that if they wanted to have children, he would need to earn what he called a 'proper' living. Instead, as a businessman, he amassed, over fifty years, a scholar's collection of books on Byzantium, the Ottoman Empire, the Armenians, the Turks, the Middle East more broadly. Upon his death he left behind hundreds of volumes, although how many of them he had read I cannot say. He left, that is, substantial traces of the life unlived, of the internal life, which as we all know is both hard to discern and the only one that matters.

And so in this sense it had been a pilgrimage for him, my trip to Istanbul, a trip he was then still well enough to applaud and appreciate. It was my own trip, too, of course – the thrill of the invitation, the excitement of setting one foot in Europe and another in Asia, the little glasses of steaming tea served on the ferries from one side of the Strait to another, the view of the passing boats from my room, the joy of wandering the mosques and Topkapi Palace alone on my day off, of negotiating the subway system with my three words of Turkish, of slipping into the plush seats at the cinema alongside a wonderfully cantankerous old American acquaintance from Boston and his deferential Turkish student, to see, of all strange things, Marjane Satrapi's *Persepolis* – no, it was my own trip too. But its ultimate raison d'être was my father.

So, too, with Beirut. My father, before ever he saw Istanbul, was a child in Beirut. Beirut was his Eden. My grandfather was first posted there as naval attaché to the French Consulate in 1936. My father was just five years old; my aunt three. They lived in a villa on an ascendance at what was then the edge of town and is now indiscernibly incorporated into the city; a place that has not only vanished but the very notion of which has vanished. It was my grandparents' first moment of relative prosperity: until then, they had been frankly poor, and only in Beirut did they have the luxury of a housekeeper. There, too, they bought their first furniture, which they would take with them to their next posting, only to have it evaporate a few years later, mid-war, when the ship carrying it belatedly back to Algeria was torpedoed in the Mediterranean.

From Beirut, in 1939, they were dispatched to Salonica. There, they heard word of the French defeat and the armistice. My grandfather – who spent a decade of his retirement writing, by hand, a 3,000-page memoir of his life for his granddaughters, for my sister and myself – records the shame and horror of this development; but he was also a follower of rules and of order, and so rather than rebel, he followed the command that then emanated from Vichy, taking him back to Beirut in 1940, and then on to Istanbul in 1941.

Their Beirut of before the war is recorded in family photographs as a time of outings and parties: the children are captured in elaborate fancy dress (my father as a court page, in red velveteen bloomers with white-and-gold brocade, complete with feathered toque; my aunt as a tiny princess, in layers of frothy skirts) among others similarly attired, all staring dumbly off into the corners of the frame, as photographed children are wont to do. The grown-ups are pictured smiling in the streets or at the St Georges Hotel on the waterfront. Their letters talk of the ease and beauty of it all, the fragrant flowers in the garden and the warmth of the local welcome. There was food enough for everyone. At the weekends, there were outings to the mountains; throughout, an abundance of fresh oranges and sweet cakes and coffee. And always, the sunshine and their beloved Mediterranean extending to the horizon.

The return to Beirut in 1941 was much darker. Food, while plentiful in comparison to other places, was considerably more difficult to procure than it had been. The children suffered from headaches and earaches and colds. Housekeepers were in short supply, as was money to pay for them. My father, now nine and stoical, lived with his family in an apartment on the Rue Achrafieh, at the summit of the hill in what is still today the Christian district. There was then a French airbase across the road. The children attended the French elementary school only a few blocks away on the corner of the Rue de Damas – the Road to Damascus – where now there stands a large modern tower containing offices, luxury apartments and shops.

My father and aunt did not know that times were worse: they knew only that they had returned to their beloved Beirut. All through the rest of the war that was their childhood, after they were back in Algiers, keeping a chicken on their tiny balcony for its eggs, until the afternoon it took alarm at the children's antics and fluttered dizzily down to the courtyard only to be slaughtered by a neighbour for supper; or queuing endlessly for rations to find that the meat – or the rice, or the butter – had run out; or hiding in the air-raid shelters overnight in the unsettled stretch when school was cancelled for weeks, and my grandmother, in hope of salvaging the year, dragged my father around to tutor after tutor – including, for Latin, an aged monk in grimy attire crammed with his parents into a small and filthy flat on the outskirts of town, with an entire flock of pigeons in cages on the porch; or being shipped out to ancient aunts in the countryside in the hope that there they would have calm and food – throughout all that time, the children spoke of Beirut as the answer. My father wrote more than once in his looped still-childish hand to his father, far away – first in Toulon, then in Dakar, then in Casa – that he wished they were back in Beirut. Beirut, where, for the children at least, everything had been good.

None of the complications of war featured in my father's Beirut – or if they did, they did so only decades later, in retrospect. My father's Beirut was his happy home, the place he could first clearly remember, where life was comfortable and Mummy and Daddy were happy and school was exciting and everything seemed to lie ahead, and to be possible. The city's perfection was always a child's myth, but a myth so perfectly imprinted that when, before I left for my own trip there, I sat next to him in the nursing home and asked him to draw a map of the city as he remembered it, he shifted in his wheelchair and closed his eyes for a moment, and then, having moved the pen back and forth above the page a few times in a hovering motion, drew a perfect outline of the city's coast and penned in the port, and the St Georges, and the American University in Ras Beirut, and the Pigeon Rocks offshore, and the Rue de Damas heading inland and uphill – all exactly as they are in life, although, since leaving in 1941, he'd only been back in Beirut for forty-eight hours some thirty years later, just before the civil war, a stopover born of a somewhat garbled matter of lost luggage on the way back from Hong Kong. When I showed the map to my Lebanese architect friend, he marvelled at its accuracy.

And then, too, my father put down in the same black ink, and of course with the same certainty, the souk where they shopped for food, and Tanios, the central department store where his mother used to take him, and the airbase across the road from his apartment building; all of these things gone now, or transformed beyond recognition, and certainly beyond caring, in a city which has suffered and survived so much in the intervening decades.

Yet even just a few months ago they existed, absolutely, in all their vividness, in my father's memory, and he could indicate them for me on a scrap of lined yellow paper and so insist upon their continued reality, their absolute importance, perfectly preserved in every detail – you do know, don't you, that in the moment in which he closed his eyes before he drew his map, he knew the quality of the light, the shadows cast by the buildings in the road, the clattering of the cars passing, and the mingling smells in the street, of cooking fat and gasoline and dirt, and the ruts in the pavement beneath the thin soles of his shoes, and the fine layer of dust upon those shoes, and the weight of the department-store door and the texture of its handle as it swung open, and the warmth, too, of his mother's hand, cold now for almost thirty years – in the precious box of his childhood mind for seven decades and finally, finally taken out unblemished, at the last, for me.

And now, these few months later, he is dead and these memories have dissolved into the ether and all that remains is the yellow slip of paper folded and already worn in the pocket of my diary, a mere desiccation, a sign stripped of its significance. Everybody thinks this, I know, but I think it now with great confusion: how can it be, that all that is in us dies with us? How can it be that those memories, that Beirut – which had existed seventy years in its locked corner of his mind, but not the less real or immediate for that – have now simply ceased to be? I cannot understand it. That we cannot know something unless we are told it: this seems to me the greatest weakness of any supposed divine plan, the primary reason to doubt.

On the afternoon when he drew his map, I asked my father whether he would like me not to go. 'All you have to do is say you'd like me to stay,' I said. 'And I will stay. I can cancel it.' I had in my head that the trip was important, somehow important for my father and in order that I might bring him some gift – not an actual gift, of course, but an emotional gift – and that this would make his parting easier. I was aware even as I had this idea in my head that it was a silly, novelistic idea and not a true thing; but then, too, on some level, even when he was so sick, I really wanted to go. I had also been with them, my parents, almost all the time for six weeks and it was hard; and he was in pain and often sour-tempered and she was growing increasingly anxious and I wasn't sure that I could do this indefinitely, this nursing thing.

My father may have read my mind. He closed his eyes again – the kind of closing that may have been thinking or may have been necessary to ride out a wave of pain, this latter a type of eye-closing I know only from childbirth – and then he said, 'No. I think – I think it's . . . important that you go.'

And so I went.

II

What did I want from Beirut? Did I think I would encounter my father there, a child of six, or nine, walking purposefully through the streets in short trousers and long socks with a lock of dark hair falling over his right eye? Surely not, although . . . Did I think I would unearth a francophone enclave for whom my father's distant childhood would also evoke something, whatever it might be, and prompt at least a ruminative conversation about the city of that period? Perhaps. And did I think I might walk on the same pavement and stand before his old apartment building and take a photograph to carry back with me to put upon his table in the nursing home in Rye Brook, New York, thereby returning to him both some scrap of his past life and some trace of its present continuation? Naively, yes. He was so certain in his mind that it all existed still somewhere that he almost made me believe. It was as if I believed I would be travelling not only across space but across time, into the very distant but perfectly preserved place he had laid out in his little map.

And at the same time: did I envisage a trip like my visit to Istanbul, in which the city was opened to me in its various marvels, past and present, and its various atrocities, too, by the generosity of my influential and devoted hosts? Yes, that certainly. I certainly imagined that I would be introduced to writers, professors, journalists and politicians, would be conducted through refugee camps and have explained to me by passionate interlocutors the history of the Nakba as it has affected Lebanon; and then the history of the civil war; and the history since the civil war; and so on. Only by imagining such a grand tour could I justify leaving him; without that, it was an abandonment.

I was, on my father's account but also simply for itself, passionately interested in Beirut. I wanted so much from it. Beirut, meanwhile, proved to be dispassionately uninterested in me. Our pilot programme, it transpired, in spite of the fancy names attached to it, was merely that: a pilot programme at the American University (a beautiful campus by the sea, and as close to a private American college as can be found outside the United States) for a two-week summer class in creative writing for undergraduates. My lovely and immensely patient poet colleague and I were furnished with a windowless classroom, a milling contingent of bright and, for the most part, motivated students, a fluorescent hum, an ugly carpet. Like so many Rapunzels, we were then locked in for three hours each morning for two weeks. The curriculum was up to us. But for a few young women in hijabs, we might have been in Allegheny or Eugene.

As for my father's history, nobody cared. Why should they? The image of my father as a child – a colonial child, so long ago – did not capture their attention even for a second. I bored my poet colleague with my insistence on my mission; and I bored my architect friend. Our hostess, raised largely in the US, nodded vaguely when I asked her about it; her husband, raised in Beirut and barely younger than my father, shrugged and turned away. The night they invited us to supper, I plagued the other dinner guests, including a Belgian woman of about my own age who was compiling for the office of tourism a walking tour of the old sights of Beirut. She, at least, promised to look at old maps: Rue Achrafieh? It should be locatable.

In the meantime, I tried to enquire about that time; but everybody – including our hostess's husband – was too young to remember. Somehow, this had not occurred to me: that if my father, at seventy-nine, was dying, so too was his generation, the people who might remember the time before Before. Besides, there had been too much pain since then; and I found that they did not want to talk about that either. The people I met were happy to discuss the rebuilding of the downtown, and how they felt about it – too Disney, or just right? Was the influence of Solidere good or bad? What about the choice to restore certain examples of colonial architecture rather than those in the Ottoman style? And in moments of greater intimacy, what did they really think about Rafic Hariri, and his reconstruction plan, and his assassination? The residents, both young and old, were keen to show off the lively downtown, and to suggest beautiful hotel bars or stylish restaurants where we might spend an evening.

This was the strangeness of Beirut: it was to me like a city in a dream, a city wiped clean. With its lovely prospect overlooking the sea, its youthful and worldly population, its expensive shops and perfectly rebuilt arcades and plazas, its surface resembles very closely someone's ideal of Beirut. Unless you poke around for a while on foot, you will not see much evidence, beyond the relentless construction, of the total destruction of their civil war – with the notable exceptions of the hulk of the Hilton hotel, a punctured and hollowed concrete misery purposefully retained as a reminder; and the smaller, squatter ruin of the St Georges on the waterfront, maintained in its decrepitude by the owner who, I was told, despised Hariri and his tidy beautification of the downtown. While I was there, a new Four Seasons opened by the water, a shiny white tower with its balconies turned to the sea, outside of which pooled glossy black limousines. Repeatedly I saw these limousines – often SUVs with Saudi or Abu Dhabi plates – pull up suddenly and eject their passengers, smooth young men on mobile phones, with white keffiyehs, holding the hems of their pristine white djellabas above the dirt as they dashed into Dunkin' Donuts or Burger King for a snack.

When I observed to my architect friend how few Western tourists I glimpsed in Beirut, he laughed. 'Nobody here cares about Western tourists,' he said. 'You come for a week, two at the most, on a tight budget. You buy nothing, and you go away again. We want tourists from the Gulf, or from elsewhere in the Middle East. We want people who will buy a villa or take a floor or two in a luxury hotel, stay for months, spend millions. That's what keeps the city booming.' Moreover, he added, 'Beirut has always been the party centre for the Middle East. You can find anything here – sex, drugs, gambling, all of it. Last year there was a Middle East Bear Convention in town – big, hairy gay guys from all over the Arab world.'

The new Beirut is a fantasy city, the place where dreams come true. Its own history – and there is so much history there, in a place where ruins are revealed at almost every construction site: not just recent ruins, but Roman ruins, or Phoenician ruins – becomes no less unreal than its present. For obvious reasons, nobody wants to talk about the past, nor even, as long as things remain quiet, about the present – the students at the American University are asked to refrain from discussing politics – and nobody who is not from there really wants to know. Instead, you can marvel at the reconstruction, superficially lament the political instability just below the surface, and sip your cocktail while admiring the spectacular views.

While in Lebanon, I made the pilgrimage to Baalbek, to the Roman ruins of what was Heliopolis, Rome's capital in the

Middle East. The city is located in the Bekaa Valley, about a hundred kilometres east of Beirut over the mountains, and features some of the best preserved Roman architecture in the world. The scale of the site and the perfection of the Temple of Dionysus in particular defy description. But perhaps what was most extraordinary of all was our sense that the ruins were ours.

For at least the first hour there, my poet friend and I were all but alone. A guide or two hovered at the entrance, smoking cigarettes and kicking dust, hoping for a job. But we were able to amble among the giant pilasters and plinths, up and down the fractured steps, under the arches and among the walls, in total silence, the sky enormous above us and the mountains, framed by the ruined arches, snow-tipped at the horizon. We slipped into history without any human interruption whatsoever. At one point we perched upon a carved boulder in the shade of a massive stone wall and, like children, ate our snack brought from home, of soggy butter biscuits and slightly salty lukewarm water. I think I even swung my feet. Looking around at the empty permanence of all these discarded stones, blocks for giants tumbled as far as the eye could see, I experienced a moment of genuine wonder: it was as if we'd discovered the ruins ourselves, as if, since the gods had abandoned their playground, no one else had seen it.

And yet, of course, this fantasy was rife with irony. Why were there, even later in that long morning, so few visitors wandering the temples at Baalbek? Could it be because for so many years, until recently indeed, it was a physically dangerous place for tourists to venture, and they did so at their peril? Even now it lies deep in Hezbollah-controlled territory, a fact brought home along the route by exuberant Hezbollah posters and statues, and chiefly by the immense murals at the site's entrance, one of them depicting Hassan Nasrallah, the leader of Hezbollah, wielding a rocket launcher beside photographs of Jerusalem, Tel Aviv, Haifa and Ben Gurion Airport under cross hairs.

The effect was of simultaneous kitsch and horror. And then there was the inevitable strange realization that this, too, was just

life, no more nor less, and that for the guide awaiting his customers
or for the crooked-toothed woman selling pitta with *za'atar* in the
street outside, the mural of Nasrallah was no stranger than, to me, a
billboard advertising McDonald's on the Massachusetts Turnpike.

Unexpectedly, this very experience of dislocation – to be a benign
tourist floating along the surface above a subterranean political
nightmare – was perhaps the closest that I came on this strange
Lebanese journey to a homage to my father, and to an inadvertent
reliving of my youth. There was a reason why my long drift through
Baalbek felt so known, from the stones against the big empty sky to
the painfully eager salesboys outside the few trinket-shop-cum-cafes
on the periphery, and the disagreeable huckster with his scraggly,
fly-infested camel, offering rides: these familiars were the extras of
my childhood.

Throughout the 1970s, our curious and surely not oblivious
father carted his wife and small children to vacations not at beachside
resorts but in impending global hot spots, usually before the shit had
officially hit the fan. I remember my mother painfully yanking my
hair into braids in a Lima hotel room before dawn, before we set out
to catch an early plane to Quito, and shouting at my father, 'This is
not my idea of a holiday!' Among other junkets, we visited Ethiopia in
1971 (we stopped also in Kenya, but the projected Ugandan portion
of that trip sadly had to be cancelled due to some trouble with a
dictator), Guatemala in 1973 (my sister and I wondered aloud why
we were the only tourists around), Sri Lanka in 1975, and so on.

My memories of these childhood travels are, in one regard at least,
not unlike my father's childhood memories of Beirut: blissful to me,
they represent an isolated gem of privileged innocence in the midst
of unacknowledged oncoming darkness. Whether that gem was a
falsehood or a strange little truth I cannot quite say. But I can see
why he would have wanted, however unconsciously, to recreate that
strange and precious state. It was, in *his* youth, the happiest state: to
be protected and only faintly aware, in the middle of *someone else's*

horror. Surely this is not a false question: is the quiet banality of a place less real than its incipient evil? Isn't life, most strangely, always made more real by its banalities?

What do I remember about Ethiopia? Not unrest or famine. Not global Cold War politics played out on an African stage – although my parents would for years tell the story of the TASS reporter who dandled me on his knee on a bus upcountry. No, I, who was five and a half years old, remember our propeller plane spitting fire from its engine ('Look, Mummy, there are flames out the window!'), landing in a field on the way to Lalibela and a squealing gaggle of children in rags running up, begging smilingly for pencils and touching my sister's blonde hair.

What do I remember of Guatemala, when I was seven? The market ladies in their vivid ponchos and mannish hats, their eyes downcast and their wares laid out, most orderly, upon blankets, in the street running down from the pristine white church in Chichicastenango.

Of Sri Lanka when I was nine, I recall the murky green swimming pool at the Holiday Inn (we could not see the bottom, which disturbed my mother, but not sufficiently to forbid us swimming in it) and the vastness of our glorious family room at the Galle Face Hotel, the biggest and most old-fashioned hotel room I'd ever seen, with its crisp linens, its dark wood and its lazy ceiling fan. I remember my sister turning cartwheels along the green sward abutting the seafront, and being given a garnet ring by our parents for her birthday.

Any possibility of bloodshed and horror is excised from my memories of these places; or rather, more accurately, my father gave us these places without horror. He gave them to us as sites of innocent joy.

This is an impossibility, of course. The very attempt is perverse, a denial of reality. But I can see now that this is what he attempted: we didn't take off to Mallorca or the Bahamas or Hawaii for our childhood holidays; and it now seems a wonder that we didn't vacation in Belfast or Santiago. What it meant to him – atonement, escapism, folly – I cannot say, nor can I now ask. But when in Beirut I leaned over my dorm-room balcony and saw a lone European mother walking her two small, fair daughters, in matching dresses, along the street, I held them in my mind until I spoke to my husband that night: 'I saw my sister and me today,' I told him. Not my father as a child, but myself.

I cannot say what drove my father, but what his lessons taught me, I realize belatedly, is to be a novelist. To understand that most of *what is*, you can only imagine, and can imagine only through the often contradictory traces of what you can see. To understand that always, at the heart of things – whatever the ideas and ideologies, the violations and violence, the peculiarities of culture – always at the heart are ordinary people, and there is just life, being lived: tables and bread and toilets and scissors and cigarettes and kisses and illness and death; just life.

III

I had been living in my American University dorm room for a week when my sister said on the telephone that my father was asking for me. I was on the balcony, speaking on the local mobile phone that I'd acquired from a dusty little shop opposite the university, peering over the balustrade at the passers-by. It was night-time, but my street in Ras Beirut did not go quiet in the evenings. The World Cup was everywhere. Every possible screen was illuminated – the green of the soccer pitch glowed in apartments and outside cafes – and cars drove hooting at all hours through the neighbourhood.

Our immediate family is small; everyone was there but me. My sister said that my father was in pain for longer stretches each day – even though they'd added a new type of painkiller, these did not seem to help very much – but that there were still good moments. He knew this would not continue for long – he'd said to my aunt that what he feared was not death but the pain – and he wanted me to be with them, for us all to be together, before the pain was too much. Before he had to go into the land of morphine, and away.

Our trip to Baalbek took place over the weekend, when I already knew I would be leaving. On the Sunday morning, I went to a local swimming club, a collection of vivid pools by the seafront near the Luna Park. Not surprisingly, I found that I could not in good conscience lounge by the chemical blue water and enjoy the hot sun and the children splashing. I was obsessively reading Rabih Alameddine's novel, *The Hakawati*, about Lebanon and a father's death, about a young man travelling from America to Beirut to stand at his father's bedside, and to try to defer his father's death by telling all the stories in the world. *Of course* that was what I was reading: a book about my father, about my calling, about Beirut. But I couldn't read it on the deckchair by the swimming pool by the sea near the Pigeon Rocks.

I experienced the spiritual equivalent of not knowing where to put your hands. I could not ignore what I knew was taking place without me. I could not fully be where I was; and even as I did not want to be in the King Street Nursing Home in Rye Brook, New York, I'd reached a point where I couldn't be anywhere else. My father could not protect me any longer, not even by sending me away; the time had come for us to join together and meet Death at last, not (as for Rabih Alameddine) in Beirut but in, as it would happen, a residential hospice in Stamford, Connecticut.

Just before I left Beirut, my kindly hostess took me to find the Rue Achrafieh. Her younger Belgian friend had located it on an old map; and we could see, in fact, that all along it had been right there on the current map as well, its trajectory largely unchanged. For a week, I had looked and hadn't been able to find it – why not? It was not a small or remote street – and nor had anybody else. It was as if it had been hidden by sorcery and only belatedly revealed.

Rue Achrafieh was a road of apartment buildings, most of them new; of one or two small villas, bearing the pockmarks of the civil war; of an unobtrusive mosque on the side where the French airbase must have been; and of large tracts of waste ground, hidden behind hoardings, from which sprouted saplings, and giant bushes that could be seen to wave their green, fronded arms. Much had been destroyed and subsequently razed. At one point, you could peer through to the next street, where stood – as in London after the Blitz – half a house, sheared down the middle like a doll's house, so you could see half a floor, and half a wall, and the flocked wallpaper at the back of the living room, and the tatters of curtains fluttering at the gaping windows. This, although the war has been over for twenty years. Here, at last, just a few blocks off the tourist route, stood evidence of the time Before. Not, alas for my father, evidence of the time before Before: his era was too long gone for that. But at least, here, I could discern the city that might have arisen after his city.

My hostess approached a group of old men playing backgammon, perched in a circle on the ubiquitous white plastic chairs in a smaller vacant lot near the top of the street. Silver-haired, they were elegant in their dress shirts and pressed trousers, idling away the afternoon; but close inspection – and an enquiry in Arabic by my hostess – revealed that while old, they weren't old enough. The eldest was perhaps in his early seventies, barely born in 1940. Their inspection of me was patient, neutral – looking me over from head to toe, accepting that I take their photograph; they weren't hostile but they weren't interested either. So much water under the bridge. They shook their heads, blew cigarette smoke out in satisfied whorls over the scrubby ground and returned to their game: my search dismissed with the flick of a hand.

On Wednesday, I flew to Paris, and thence to New York. I arrived in time to celebrate my aunt's birthday, a day after my father's. Of course, when I gave them to him, my father didn't care about the posters of old Beirut that I had brought, or even about the photographs of Rue Achrafieh (in a quick glance, nothing looked familiar, to him or to my aunt). He sampled only the tiniest crumb of his beloved halva. By then, he'd travelled already too far along his road – as it were – to Damascus.

So began the end of the end. One day soon thereafter, he insisted on getting up to sit by the window, for what would be the last time. 'Why, Daddy?' I asked. 'If it hurts, stay in bed.'

'Because I don't want to miss –' he gestured at the wide world through the plate glass – 'all this.' Which says everything, really, about my father and his life.

But the pain, by then, was too great; and the call for relief too intense. He was transferred to the hospital the next day; and a day later to the hospice; and when next I saw him, he was asleep, in the blissful release, the terminal sleep, of morphine. He opened his eyes to smile and wave at the children – his particular fluttering of his stubby fingers, with his hand held up to his cheek. Later again, he opened his eyes to speak once more to his wife. He whispered, without opening his eyes, of my sister.

And on the last morning, as he slept so sweetly, as placid as a child at last, after a day of thrashing and fretting and rattling, I held tightly his safe, warm hand – although it felt, as it always had, as though he held mine – and wished him Godspeed on his journey: not to my Beirut, but, inshallah, perhaps to his, to the pellucid safety and hope of before Before, a place for which I have, in my diary, his neatly folded map, but to which I can never go. ■

Endpapers

I

If the road's a frayed ribbon strung through dunes
continually drifting over
if the night grew green as sun and moon
changed faces and the sea became
its own unlit unlikely sound
consider yourself lucky to have come
this far   Consider yourself
a trombone blowing unheard
tones   a bass string plucked or locked
down by a hand its face articulated
in shadow, pressed against
a chain-link fence   Consider yourself
inside or outside, where-
ever you were when knotted steel
stopped you short   You can't flow through
as music or
as air

II

What holds what binds is breath   is
primal vision in a cloud's eye
is gauze around a wounded head
is bearing a downed comrade out beyond
the numerology of vital signs
into predictless space

III

The signature to a life requires
the search for a method
rejection of posturing
trust in the witnesses
a vial of invisible ink
a sheet of paper held steady
after the end-stroke
above a deciphering flame

GRANTA

THIRTY GIRLS

Susan Minot

The night they took the girls, Sister Giulia went to bed with only the usual amount of worry and foreboding and rubbing of her knuckles. She said her extra prayer that all would stay peaceful, twisted down the rusted dial of her kerosene lamp and tucked in the loose bit of mosquito net under the mattress.

The bed was small and she took up very little of it, being a slight person barely five feet long. Indeed, seeing her asleep one might have mistaken her for one of her twelve-year-old students and not the forty-two-year-old headmistress of a boarding school that she was. Despite her position, Sister Giulia's room was one of the smaller rooms upstairs in the main building at St Mary's where the sisters were housed. Sisters Alba and Fiamma shared the largest room down the hall and Sister Rosario – who simply took up more space with her file cabinets and seed catalogues – had commandeered the room with the shallow balcony overlooking the interior walled garden. But Sister Giulia didn't mind. She was schooled in humility and it came naturally to her.

The banging appeared first in her dream.

When she opened her eyes she knew immediately it was real and as present in the dark room as her own beating heart. It entered the open window, a rhythmic banging like dull axes hitting at stone. She thought, They are at the dorms.

Then she heard a softer knocking at her door. She was already sitting up, her bare feet feeling for the straw flip-flops on the floor. Yes? she whispered.

Sister, said a voice, and in the darkness she saw the crack in the door widen and in it the silhouetted head of the nightwatchman.

George, I am coming, she said, and felt for the cotton sweater on the chair beside her table. Sister, the voice said. They are here.

She stepped into the hall and met with the other nuns whispering in a shadowy cluster. At the end of the hallway one window reflected dim light from the two floodlights at the main entrance. The women moved towards it like moths. Sister Alba already had her habit on – she was never uncovered – and Sister Giulia wondered in the lightning way of idle thoughts if Sister Alba slept in her habit, and then thought of how preposterous it was to be having that thought at this moment.

Che possiamo fare? said Sister Rosario. What to do? Sister Rosario usually had an opinion on exactly what to do but now, in a crisis, was deferring to her superior.

We cannot fight them, Sister Giulia said, speaking in English for George.

No, no, the nuns mumbled, agreeing, even Sister Rosario.

They must be at the dormitory, someone said.

Yes, Sister Giulia said. I think this, too. Let us pray the door holds.

They listened to the banging. Now and then a voice shouted, a man's voice.

Sister Chiara whispered from the back. The door must hold.

It was bolted from the inside with a big steel beam. When the sisters had put the girls to bed they waited to hear the giant plank slide into place before saying goodnight.

Andiamo, Sister Giulia said. We must not stay here, they would find us. Let us hide in the garden and wait. What else can we do?

Everyone shuffled mouse-like down the back stairs. On the ground floor they crossed the tiled hallway past the canning rooms and closed door of the storage room and into the laundry past the tables and wooden shelves. Sister Alba was breathing heavily. Sister Rosario jangled the keys, unlocking the laundry, and they stepped outside to the cement walkway bordering the sunken garden. A clothes line hung nearby with a line of pale dresses followed by a line of pale T-shirts. Dark paths divided the garden in crosses, and in between were humped tomato plants and the darker clumps of coffee leaves and white lilies bursting like trumpets. A three-quarter moon in the western sky cast a grey light over all the foliage so it looked covered in talc.

The nuns huddled against the far wall under banana trees. The wide leaves cast moonlit shadows.

The banging, it does not stop, whispered Sister Chiara. Her hand was clamped over her mouth.

They are trying very hard, Sister Alba said.

We should have moved them, Sister Rosario said. I knew it.

The headmistress replied in a calm tone. Sister, we cannot think of this now.

They'd put up the outside fence two years ago, and last year they'd been given the soldiers. Government troops came, walking around campus with guns strapped across their chests, among the bougainvillea and girls in their blue uniforms. At night some were stationed at the end of the driveway passing through the empty field, some stood at the gate near the chapel. Then, a month ago, the army had a census-taking and the soldiers were moved twenty kilometres north. Sister Giulia had pestered the commander to send the soldiers back. There were warnings of an attack – never more than a day's warning when the rumours would reach them – so the nuns took the girls to nearby homes for the night. They will be back, the commander said. Finally last week the soldiers returned. The girls slept, the sisters slept. Then came the holiday on Sunday. The commander said, They will be back at the end of the day. But they didn't return. They stayed off in the villages, getting drunk on sorghum beer.

The jeep had been out of fuel so Sister Giulia took the bicycle to Atoile. Where was the army? From Atoile someone went all the way to Loro in Kamden to see if they were there. No sign of the soldiers. She sent a message to Salim Salee, the commander of the North, who was in Gulu. Must we close the school? she asked. No, do not close the school, he answered by radio. When she arrived back at St Mary's it was eight o'clock and pitch-black and still nothing was settled. Sister Alba had the uneaten dinner there waiting for the soldiers. Sister Rosario had overseen the holiday celebrations and gathered the girls at the dorm for an early lights-out.

The banging had now become muted. The garden where the nuns stayed hiding was still, but the banging and shouting reached them, travelling over the quadrangle, then the roof. Across the leafy paths by the main entrance they could see George's shadow where he'd positioned himself, holding a club.

I don't hear any of the girls, said Sister Fiamma.

No, said Sister Giulia. They could make out each other's faces, and Sister Giulia's eyebrows were pointed toward one another as they often were, in a concerned peak.

What's burning? Sister Guarda pointed over the roof to a braid of red sparks curling upward.

It's coming from the chapel, I think.

They wouldn't burn the chapel.

Sister, they murder children, these people.

They heard the tinkling of glass and the banging stopped. Instead of being a relief, the sound of only shouting – of orders being given – and the occasional sputtering of fire was more ominous.

I still do not hear the girls, said Sister Chiara. She said it in a hopeful way.

They waited for something to change. It seemed they waited a long time.

The shouts had dropped to a low calling back and forth and finally the nuns heard the voices moving closer. They were crossing the quadrangle toward the front gates. They were nearby. The nuns' faces were all turned toward George where he stood, motionless against the whitewashed wall. Sister Giulia held the crucifix on her necklace, muttering prayers.

The noise of the rebels passed. The sound grew dim. Sister Giulia stood.

Wait, Sister Alba said. We must be sure they are gone.

I can wait no longer. Sister Giulia took small steps on the shaded pathway and got to George.

Are they gone?

It appears so, George said. You remain here while I see.

No, George. She followed him on to the platform. They are my girls.

He looked at her to show he did not agree, but he was never going to argue with her. Behind her he saw the pale figures of the sisters moving from the other side of the garden like a fog. You walk behind me, he said.

George unbolted the doors of the breezeway and opened them to the gravel drive lit by the floodlights. They looked upon a devastation.

The ground was littered with trash, burned sticks and bits of rubber and broken glass. Scattered across the grass of the quadrangle in the shadows were blankets and clothes. George and Sister Giulia stepped out, emerging like figures from a spaceship on to a new planet. In front of the chapel the jeep was a roiling ball of fire, and smoke bellowed in long tubes out of smashed windows of the chapel itself. But they turned towards the dormitory. They could see a great black gap in the side where the barred windows had been. The whole frame had been ripped out and used as a ladder. That's how they'd gotten in.

Bits of glass glittered on the grass. There was torn plastic rope and deflated plastic bags. The second dormitory further down was dark and still. Thank the Lord that appeared untouched. Those were the youngest ones.

The girls . . . Sister Giulia said. She had her hands out in front of her as if testing the silence. She saw no movement anywhere.

We must look, George said.

They stood at the gaping hole with the torn-out window bars leaning up to it. The concrete around the frame was hacked away in chunks. One light shone from the back of the dormitory, the other bulbs had been smashed.

From the bushes they heard a soft voice, Sister.

Sister Giulia turned and bent down. Two girls crouched in the darkness, hugging their nightshirts.

You are here, she said, dizzy and grateful. She embraced the girls, feeling their thin arms, their small backs. The smaller one – it was Penelope – stayed clutching on.

You are safe, Sister Giulia said.

No, Penelope said, pressing her head against her stomach. We are not.

The other girl, Olivia Oki, rocked back and forth, holding her arm in pain.

Sister Giulia gathered them up and steered them out of the bushes into the light. Penelope kept a tight hold around her waist. Her face was streaked with grime and her eyes glassed over.

Sister, they took all of us, she said.

They took all of you?

Penelope nodded, crying.

Sister Giulia looked at George, whose face understood. All the girls were gone. The sisters caught up with them.

Sister Chiara embraced Penelope, lifting her. There, there, she said. Sister Fiamma was inspecting Olivia Oki's arm and now Olivia was crying too.

They tied us together and led us away, Penelope said, sobbing close to Sister Chiara's face. Later they would learn that Penelope had been raped as she tried to run across the grass and was caught near the swing.

Sister Giulia's lips were pursed into a tighter line than usual.

George, she said, make sure the fire is out. Sister Rosario, you find out how many girls are gone. I am going to change. There is no time to lose.

No more moving tentatively, no more discovering the damage, assessing what remained. She strode past Sister Alba who was carrying buckets of water toward the chapel.

Sister Giulia re-entered the nuns' quarters and took the stairs to her room. No lights were on but it was no longer pitch-black. She removed her nightdress and put on her T-shirt, then the grey dress with a collar. She tied on her sneakers, thin-soled ones that had been sent from Italy.

She hurried back down the stairs and across the entryway, ignoring the sounds of calamity around her and the smell of fire and oil and smoke. She went directly to her office and removed the lace doily from the safe under the table, turned the dial right then left and opened the thick weighty door. She groped around for the shoebox and pulled out a rolled wad of bills. She took one of the narrow paper bags they used for coffee beans and put the cash in it, then put the bag in a small backpack she removed from the hook on the door. About to leave, she noticed she'd forgotten her habit and looked around the room, like a bird looking for an insect, alert and thoughtful. She went to her desk drawer, remembering the blue scarf there. She covered her hair with the scarf, tying it at her neck, hooking it over her ears. That would have to do.

When she came out again she met with Thomas Bosco, the math teacher. Bosco, as everyone called him, was a bachelor who lived at the school and spent Christmas with the sisters and was part of the family. He stayed in a small hut off the chapel on his own. He may not have been so young but he was dependable and they could call upon him to help jump-start the jeep, replace a light bulb or deliver a goat.

Bosco, she said. It has happened.

Yes, he said. I've seen.

Sister Rosario came bursting forward with an affronted air. They have looted the chapel, she said. As usual she was making it clear she took bad news harder than anyone else.

Bosco looked at the knapsack. You are ready?

Yes. Sister Giulia nodded as if this had all been discussed. Let us go get our girls.

Bosco nodded. If it must be, let us go die for our girls.

And off they set.

By the time they had left the gate and crossed the open field of the dirt driveway and were on the path leading off into the bush, the sky had started to lighten. The silhouette of the trees emerged black against the screen. The birds had not yet started up but they would any minute. Bosco led the way, reminding the sister that they had to beware of mines. The ground was still dark and now and then they came across the glint of a crushed soda can or a candy wrapper suspended in the grass. A pale shape lay off to the side, stopping Sister Giulia's heart for a moment. Bosco bent down and picked up a small white sweater.

We are going the right way, she said. She folded the sweater and put it in her backpack and they continued on. They did not speak of what had happened or what would happen, thinking only of finding the girls.

They came to an area of a few straw-roofed huts and asked a woman bent in the doorway. Have they passed this way? She pointed further down the path. No one had telephones, yet information travelled swiftly in the bush, though it was dangerous to report on the rebels' location. When rebels discovered informants, they would cut off their lips. A path led them to a marshy area with dry reeds sticking up like masts sunk in the still water. They waded in and immediately the water rose to their chests. Sister Giulia thought of the smaller girls and how they could have made it. Not all the children could swim.

Birds began to sing, their chirps sounding particularly sweet and clear on this terrible morning. They walked on the trampled path after wringing out their wet clothes. Sister Giulia had been in this country now for five years and still the countryside felt new and beautiful to her. Mostly it was a tangle of low brush, tight and grey in the dry season, flushing out green and leafy during the rains. An acacia tree made a scrollwork ceiling above them, and on the ground yellow flowers swam like little fish among the shadows.

They met a farmer who let them know without saying anything that they were going in the right direction and further along a woman carrying branches on her head who stopped and indicated with serious eyes that, yes, this was the right way. People did not dare speak.

The sun rose, bright yellow behind them. Sister Giulia saw the figure of a person crouching in the grass at the far side of a clearing. Suddenly the person was running toward them. It was a girl. As she came closer they saw it was Irene. She was wearing her skirt as a shirt to cover her upper body. Sister Giulia embraced her and asked her if she was all right. Yes, Irene said, crying quietly. Now she was all right.

We are going to bring back the girls, Sister Giulia told her. Irene nodded with disbelief. Sister Giulia gave her the sweater from her backpack and walked back with her until they met again the woman carrying the branches, and she let Irene go with her back to a village. You found a child, you sent her off with a stranger to safety. It struck Sister Giulia how quickly one could adjust to a new way of things. But then it was simply another example of God watching over her.

Soon the sky was bright. They kept walking for an hour, then another. By now their clothes were dry though her sneakers stayed wet. The sun was high over their heads.

Far off they heard a shot and stopped, hopeful and frightened at the same time. They waited but heard nothing more. The sound had come from up ahead and they started off again with increased energy.

Sister Giulia apologized to Bosco for not having brought water. This is not important, he said.

At one point she spotted a white rectangle on the path in front of her and picked it up. It was one of the girls' identity cards. *Akello Esther*, it said. She was in the 4th Class and had recently won the essay contest for a paper on her father and the effect of his accident on their family. She showed Bosco. He nodded. They were on the right track.

When they heard shots again there were more shots and closer. Shouting voices floated through the bush from far off. They'd crossed a flat area and were now going up and down shallow hills. At the top of a higher hill they had a vista across a valley to a slope on the other side.

I see them, Bosco said. She stood near him and looked and could see only brown and green lumps with dark shadows slashed off them.

She looked further up the slope, bare of trees, and saw small bushes moving. Then she saw the girls, a line of them very close together, with white shirts and dark heads. Alongside the line were grey and green figures, larger, on either side. It was much too far to see any faces.

For a moment she couldn't believe her eyes. They'd found them. She asked herself, What am I to do now? At the same time she set off again, this time in front of Bosco. She had no plan. She prayed that God would guide her.

They took small steps down the steep path, almost immediately losing sight of the opposite slope. They moved quickly, forgetting they were tired. It was past noon and they moved in and out of a dim shade. At the bottom of the hill they could look up and see the rebels with the girls. It appeared they had stopped. It was one thing to spot them far away and another to see them closer with faces and hats and guns. Then a rebel looked down and saw her approaching and called out. She thought it was in Acholi but she couldn't tell. She held her hands up in the air and behind her Bosco did the same.

Other rebels looked over. She knew at least she would not be mistaken for an informant or an army soldier. Then she saw the girls catch sight of her. A large man walked down from higher up and stopped to watch her coming. He had yellow braid on his green shirt, a hat with a brim and no gun. He shouted to his soldiers to allow her to approach, and Sister Giulia made her way up the hill to where he waited with large arms folded. She saw the girls out of the corner of her eye, gathered now beneath a tree, and instinct told her not to look in their direction.

You are welcome, the man said. I am Captain Mariano Lagira. He did not address himself to Bosco. Sister Giulia lowered her gaze to hide her surprise at such a greeting.

She introduced herself and Thomas Bosco. I am the headmistress of St Mary's of Aboke, she said.

He nodded. She looked at him now and saw badly pockmarked skin and small eyes in a round face.

I have come for my girls, she said.

Captain Lagira smiled. Where were you last night?

I was not there, she said. Yes, it was a small lie. I had to take a sick nun to Lira. She slipped her backpack off and took out the brown bag. Here, I have money.

Mariano Lagira took the paper bag and looked inside. We don't want money. He handed the bag to a rebel who nevertheless carried it away. Follow me, he said. I will give you your girls.

She felt a great lifting in her heart. Bosco hung back under the guard of a boy who looked no older than twelve. He wore a necklace of bullets and had a hard face. She followed Lagira and as she passed closer to a group of girls started to greet them, but they remained looking down. She noticed that one rebel dressed in camouflage had a woman's full bosom.

Captain Lagira pointed to a log with a plastic bag on it. Sit here.

She sat.

What have you there?

My rosary, she said. I am praying.

Lagira fished into the pocket of his pants and pulled out a string of brown beads. Look, he said. I pray too. They both knelt down, and the rebels around them watched as the nun and the commander prayed together.

It was past noon now and the air was still. When they finished praying, Sister Giulia dared to ask him, Will you give me my girls?

Captain Lagira looked at her. Perhaps he was thinking.

Please, let them go.

This is a decision for Kony.

Joseph Kony was their leader. They called themselves the Lord's Resistance Army though it was never clear to her exactly what they were resisting. Museveni's government, she supposed, based in the South, though rebel activities remained limited to looting villages, maiming and murdering civilians and kidnapping children in the North.

The captain stood. I must send a message then, he said. He had the rebels spread out batteries in the sun to be charged and they waited. She managed for a second here and there to sneak glances at the girls and saw most of their faces tipped down but a few watching her. Would you like some tea? the captain said. She could hardly answer and at that moment they heard the sound of helicopters far off.

Suddenly everyone was moving and shouting. Hide! Cover yourselves, they yelled. Sister Giulia saw people grabbing branches and the girls looked as if they were being thrashed as they were covered. She was pulled over to duck under bushes. Some of the girls had moved closer to her now. Leaves pressed on her. Then the loud helicopters were overhead, blowing dust off the ground and whipping the small leaves and loose dirt. Gunshots came firing down. One of the girls threw herself on Sister Giulia to protect her. It was Judith, the head girl.

The Ugandan Army patrolled the area. Sister Giulia thought, They're coming for the girls! But nearly immediately the helicopter swooped off and its blades hummed into the distance. They could not have known, it was just a routine strike. No one moved right away, waiting to be sure they were gone. After a pause, heads lifted from the ground, their cheeks lightened by the dust. Sister Giulia saw Esther Akello with her arms over her friend Agnes Ochiti. Another girl, Jessica, was wiping blood from her neck.

Orders were given now to move, quickly. The girls were tied to one another with a rope and walked in single file behind Sister Giulia. At least I am with my girls, she thought. She wondered if they would kill her. She wondered it distantly, not really believing it, but thinking it would happen whether she believed it or not. And if so, it was God's will. They walked for a couple of hours. She worried that the girls were hungry and exhausted. She saw no sign they'd been given food.

At one point she was positioned to walk along beside Mariano. She had not dared ask him many of the questions she had. But since they had prayed together she felt she could ask him one. She said, Mariano Lagira, why do you take the children?

He looked down at her, with a bland face which said this was an irritating but acceptable question. To increase our family, he said, as if this were obvious. Kony wants a big family. Then he walked ahead away from her.

After several hours they came to a wooded place with huts and round burned areas with pots hanging from rods. It looked as if further along there were other children, and other rebels. She saw where the girls were led and allowed to sit down.

Captain Lagira brought Sister Giulia over to a hut and sat on a stool. There was one guard with a gun who kept himself a few feet away from Lagira. This rebel wore a shirt with the sleeves cut off and a gold chain and never looked straight at Lagira, but always faced in his direction. He stood now behind. During the walk they had talked about prayer and about God and she learned that his God had some things not in common with her God, but Sister Giulia did not point this out. She thought it best to try to continue this strange friendship. Would Sister Giulia join him for tea and biscuits? Captain Lagira wanted to know.

She would not refuse. A young woman in a wrapped skirt came out from the hut, carrying a small stump for Sister Giulia to sit on. It was possible this was one of his wives, though he did not greet her. At the edge of the doorway she saw a hand and half of a face looking out. Tea, he said.

The woman went back into the hut and after some time returned with a tray and mugs and a box of English biscuits. They drank their tea. Sister Giulia was hungry but she did not eat a biscuit.

I ask you again, she said. Will you give me my girls. She didn't phrase it as a question.

He smiled. Don't worry, I am Mariano Lagira. He put down his mug. Now you go wash. Another girl appeared, this one a little younger, about twenty, with bare feet and small pearl earrings. She silently led Sister Giulia behind the hut to a basin of water and a plastic shower bag hanging from a tree. She must have been another wife. Sister Giulia washed her hands and face. She washed her feet and cleaned the blisters she'd gotten from her wet sneakers.

She returned to Mariano. This rebel commander was now Mariano to her, as if a friend. He still sat on his stool, holding a stick and scratching in the dirt by his feet. She glanced at the girls and saw that some of them had moved to a different place off to the side.

Mariano didn't look up when he spoke.

There are 139 girls, he said, and traced the number in the dirt.

That many, she thought, saying nothing. More than half the school.

I give you – he wrote the number by his boot as he said, 1-0-9. And I – he scratched another number – keep thirty.

Sister Giulia looked toward the girls with alarm. There was a large group on the left and a smaller group on the right. While she had been washing they were being divided. She knelt down in front of Mariano.

No, she said. They are my girls. Let them go and keep me instead.

Only Kony decides these things.

Then let me speak with Kony.

No one ever saw Kony. He was hidden over the border in Sudan. Maybe the government troops couldn't reach him there. Maybe, as some thought, President Museveni did not try so hard to find him. The North was not such a priority for Museveni and neither was the LRA. There were government troops, yes, but the LRA was not so important.

Let the girls go and take me to Kony.

You can ask him, he said, and shrugged.

Did he mean it?

You can write him a note. Captain Lagira called and a woman with a white shirt and ragged pink belt was sent to another hut, returning eventually with a pencil and piece of paper. Sister Giulia leaned the paper on her knee and wrote:

> Dear Mr Kony,
> Please be so kind as to allow Captain Mariano Lagira to
> release the girls of Aboke.
> Yours in God,
> Sister Giulia de Angelis

As she wrote each letter she felt her heart sink down. Kony would never see this note.

Y ou go write the names of the girls there, he said.
Please, Mariano, she said softly.

You do like this or you will have none of the girls, said Captain Mariano Lagira.

She left him and went over to the girls sitting on the hard ground in feathery shadows. She held the pencil and paper limply in her hand. The girls looked at her, each with meaning in her eyes.

She bent down to speak, Girls, be good . . . but she couldn't finish her sentence.

The girls started to cry. They understood everything. An order was shouted out and immediately some rebels standing nearby began grabbing branches and hitting at the girls. One jumped on the back of Louise. She saw them slap Janet. The girls became quiet.

Sister Giulia didn't know what to do. Then it seemed as if they were all talking to her at once, in low voices, whispering. No, not all. Some were just looking at her.

Please, they were saying, Sister. Take me. Jessica said, I have been hurt. Another: My two sisters died in a car accident and my mother is sick. Charlotte said, Sister, I have asthma.

Sister, I am in my period.

Sister Giulia looked back at the captain standing with his arms crossed. He was shaking his head. She said she was supposed to write their names but she was unable. The head girl, Judith, took the pencil from her and the paper and started to write.

Akello, Esther . . .

Ochiti, Agnes . . .

Judith . . . Catherine . . . Louise. Janet, Lily, Charlotte, Jessica, Angela . . .

D id I mistreat you, Sister?
No, sir.

Did I mistreat the girls?

No, sir.

So next time I come to the school, do not run away. The captain laughed. Would the Sister like more tea and biscuits? No, thank you. They bid each other goodbye. It was as if they might have been old friends.

You may go greet them before you go, Mariano Lagira said.

Sister Giulia once again went over to the thirty girls, her thirty girls who would not be coming with her. She gave her rosary to Judith and said, Look after them. She handed Jessica her own sweater out of the backpack.

When we go you must not look at us, she said.

No, Sister, we won't.

Then a terrible thing happened.

Catherine whispered, Sister. It's Agnes. She has gone, just over there.

Sister Giulia saw Agnes standing with the larger group of girls gathered to leave.

You must get her, Sister Giulia said. She couldn't believe she was having to do this. If they see one is missing . . .

So Agnes was brought back. She was carrying a pair of sneakers. She was told she was endangering the others.

OK, Agnes said. I will not try to run away again.

Sister Giulia had to make herself turn to leave.

Charlotte called after her, Sister, are you coming back for us?

Sister Giulia left with the large group of girls. They walked away into the new freedom of the same low trees and scruffy grasses that now had a new appearance, and left the thirty others behind. Bosco led the way and Sister Giulia walked in the middle. Some girls came up beside her and held her hand for a while. They bowed their heads when she passed near them. Arriving at a road they turned on to it. The rebels stayed off the roads. It grew dark and they kept walking. They came to a village that was familiar to some of them and ended up stopping at two houses where they spent the night. There were fifty girls grouped at each house, so most of them lay outside, sleeping close in one another's arms. Sister Giulia felt she was awake all night, but then somehow her eyes were opening and it was dawn.

At 5 a.m. they fetched water and continued the journey home. As the birds started up they were within distance of the school and found that word had been sent ahead, and in little areas they passed people who were clapping as they went by. Sister Giulia felt some happiness in the welcome but inside there was still distress. They came finally to their own road and at last on to the school drive.

Across the field Sister Giulia caught sight of the crowd of people near the gate. The parents were all there waiting. She saw the chapel blackened behind the purple bougainvillea but the tower above was still standing.

Many girls ran out to embrace their mothers who were hurrying to them. As she got close, Sister Giulia saw the parents' faces watching, the parents still looking for their daughters. They searched the crowd. There was Jessica's mother with her hand holding her throat. She saw Louise's mother Grace ducking side to side, studying the faces of the girls. The closer they got to the gate, the more the girls were engulfed by their families and the more separated became the adults whose children were not there. The families held each other and kept their attention away from the parents whose girls had been left behind. They would not meet their gaze. In this way those parents learned their children had not made it back. When they came near Sister Giulia, in all the commotion even she turned away. She was answering other questions. Some mothers knelt in front of her, some kissed her hand. She was thinking only of those other parents, and she would talk to them eventually, but just now it seemed impossible to face them. Then she wondered if she'd be able to face anyone again ever. ■

Join
The Royal Society
of Literature

When you consider the wealth of national and international culture it delivers, an RSL membership isn't just a bargain, it's worth the world.
Ali Smith

Membership of The Royal Society of Literature is open to all.

For full information about the benefits of membership and how to join:
Telephone 020 7845 4677
Email rachel@rslit.org
Website www.rslit.org

GRANTA

CITY BOY

Judy Chicurel

The headline on page three read: FOSTER BOY TURNS KILLER, KILLS SELF, and I would have missed it if I hadn't seen the photo. Even in that grainy texture there was no mistaking the eyes, but still I scanned the page for a name. Stephen Schaeffer, the article said. It was him. I pulled out my cellphone, called my editor, told her I'd be late for the meeting. Then I sat down on the steps of St Michael's Church. I had quit smoking six years ago, except for an occasional cigarette after I'd had a few drinks, but suddenly I wanted one so badly I could taste it. Some kids were walking by on their way to school and I paid one of them a dollar for a Marlboro Light. I lit up, coughed twice, and continued reading.

It was in another life that I'd known him, ten years ago, when I lived on East 7th Street, between First and Avenue A, a section famous for winning Block Association awards because the windows of the brownstones sparkled in the sunlight. (Rain or shine, cold or sweltering, the Ukrainian women were out there, cleaning them with newspapers and vinegar.) I was involved with a writer who kept empty milk cartons in his refrigerator. He, in turn, was in love with a short girl who lived in Rhode Island, who'd stopped seeing him because she felt his lifestyle was unstable. I was drinking too much and working part-time at the Yiddish Actors' Association on 2nd Street. The building had, at one time, been a theatre, and now the upstairs floors were rented to the Pantheon Palace, which featured strip shows and dancing girls who arranged themselves in small booths lined with black velvet.

I worked in the Public Relations Department, where Meyer Lubkin, our boss, spent his days mourning the death of the Yiddish Theatre and trying to get Isaac Bashevis Singer on the phone to write something for the few faded stars still around, like Luba Kadison and Stella Adler. Every Friday, he stood before the open window, lamenting, 'Where are the Jews? Where are the Jews? What's to become of us? I'm ruined!'

On Fridays, we got out early for Shabbat, and Ophelia, the receptionist, and I would smoke a joint while sitting on the stone wall by the New York City Marble Cemetery, where James Lenox, founder of the New York Public Library, was buried, along with a prosperous merchant named Preserved Fish, a fact we found absolutely hilarious when we were properly stoned. We'd then go to a bar on Second Avenue to drink vodka tonics that tasted rancid because the glasses were dirty. I was in my mid-twenties and exhausted by the drama of my life, and after seeing a posting on the Met Foods bulletin board, I decided to volunteer at the Thorns of Christ Home for Forgotten Children, a glorified orphanage on Houston Street. I felt that since moving to the city I was living a lost life, and hoped that hanging out with children would help me find something useful.

The vetting process turned out to be an exhaustive affair, involving fingerprints and references and orientations and TB tests. Sister Katherine Sage, who everyone called Sister K, wore PF Flyers with her traditional habit, and coordinated the volunteer programme at Thorns of Christ, or Thorny, as it was commonly called. The way it worked, you were assigned a child and expected to spend eight hours per month with him or her, in supervised group settings on the grounds of Thorny, for the first three months. After that, you could go on one-on-one outings, as long as the proposed activity was approved at least a week in advance.

'Say your child doesn't like you,' Sister K said at the orientation. 'Well, so what? Everyone can't like everyone. We expect you to make an effort, but after the first three visits, if you're experiencing difficulty forming a connection, you must let us know and in no way feel that it's your fault. Suffering is not part of this programme, for you or the children.'

He was almost six years old when I met him, that first day in the shabby living room. I was disappointed that he was so young; I had hoped for one of the older kids because I had a degree in secondary education and was on the Board of Education's list for substitute teaching. But I was usually too hungover when they called to offer an assignment. He was big for his age, tall, wiry, with a blond buzz cut and huge blue eyes fringed by black lashes, wearing too-big jeans, a too-tight red-and-blue-striped rugby shirt and a wary, watchful expression. He folded his arms across his chest when I tried to shake hands and rolled his eyes when I suggested that we sit down and get acquainted, as many of the other volunteers were doing. I learned that he liked dogs and snakes but hated cats and alligators; liked peanut butter and strawberry-jam sandwiches but hated grape jelly; loved pizza and brownies but hated string beans. When time was up, he still wouldn't shake my hand, and when I said I was looking forward to seeing him next week, he shook his head as though I was an idiot.

Sister K encouraged the volunteers to visit at least weekly, if possible, 'to give the children something to look forward to'. I never had the impression that Stevie looked forward to seeing me or spending time with me; he still refused to shake hands but agreed to play game after game of checkers, at which he excelled.

I worried that he didn't like me. I tried discussing it with the writer, who sighed, said, 'Ah, kids,' and turned his attention to the Mets game on television. Ophelia thought I was nuts. 'He's a kid, for Christsake, who cares if he likes you.' She wasn't enthusiastic about the volunteer programme anyway, because on the days I participated I wasn't available to smoke a joint or go drinking at the nameless bar on the corner. Ophelia had grown up in the projects, surrounded by single mothers and screaming kids, and wanted no part of it.

I discussed it with Dixie, one of the dancers from the Pantheon Palace whom I'd come to know from going up on the roof to smoke cigarettes; Meyer's wife had died of emphysema and he forbade smoking in the office. Dixie was tall and slender with a great mane of curly brown hair, and always wore killer heels and blood-red lipstick. I had mentioned my involvement in the volunteer programme casually, but she became interested and asked me how it was going more frequently than I would have expected.

'Whyntcha bring him a toy or something, something little boys like, you know, a GI Joe doll or something?' she suggested. But we weren't allowed to bring presents for the kids. Sister K said we shouldn't try to buy their affections or attention with bribes.

Dixie wrinkled her nose. 'What kind of half-assed rule is that?' she asked. 'Kids love presents. Shit, who doesn't? But listen to me,' she said wistfully, with a self-deprecating laugh. 'Like I know what the fuck I'm talking about.' She was bathed in the musky heat of Indian summer that surrounded the city, a rose-and-golden glow that illuminated her pale skin and wild hair as she stood against the backdrop of the broken sign that advertised 'Girls! Girls! Girls!', a blurred invitation to men with no place to go and nobody to hold them.

By the fourth session, I was ready to tell Sister K that Stevie and I were having trouble connecting. I was having my problems with the rebound writer and there was a limit to how much rejection I could take. I had thought this would fill a void in my life and make me feel virtuous, but instead it was creating another one and leaving me feeling disappointed and discouraged.

But that afternoon, Stevie greeted me with a question.

'What's a whore?' he asked me in his gravelly little voice, looking faintly troubled.

'Did someone call you that?' I asked him.

'Jo-Jo called my mother that,' he said.

'And who is Jo-Jo?' I asked, stalling for time. He turned, surveyed the room, and pointed to a loud, chubby boy I had noticed before because he was bossy with the other children. He looked about seven years old.

'So, what, out of the blue he up and called your mother a whore?' I asked.

'He said the reason I'm here is that my mother's a whore and she didn't want me,' he explained patiently. 'What does it mean?'

'A whore is someone who gets paid to spend time with men,' I said. What else was I going to say? He was only six years old.

He considered that. 'Is it bad?' he asked. 'Jo-Jo says that she'll burn in hell.'

'Did you – do you remember your mother?' I asked him. Sister K had told us it was a policy at Thorns of Christ not to divulge a child's history, even if it wasn't confidential information. They didn't want to prejudice anyone by revealing certain aspects of a child's life. She said the histories were usually sad and varied: infants literally left on the doorstep; babies born addicted to crack; older children abandoned in burned-out tenements, found by cops or social workers.

Stevie shook his head. 'I don't think I do,' he said regretfully. 'Sister said she was too sick to take care of me and gave me to God instead.'

'Well, what that really means is that she loved you a lot and knew that they'd take good care of you here at Thorny,' I said.

'Was she pretty?' he asked me.

'Well, I never met her,' I said. 'But I bet she was very pretty, because you're a good-looking guy.'

He considered this, but then came that troubled, almost fearful look in his eyes. 'But Jo-Jo says –' and I could see how he felt about his mother, even though he'd never known her. I remembered how I'd felt about my own mother when I was little, when I loved her so much that had she gone away and never come back, I would not have been able to bear it.

I squatted down so that I was at eye level with him.

'Listen,' I said. 'Has Jo-Jo ever met your mother? No. He doesn't know anything about her. So why are we listening to anything Jo-Jo says?'

He looked at me, weighing things, his fringed eyes boring into my brain, and finally decided that I was bigger than Jo-Jo so I must know what I was talking about.

'I hate Jo-Jo!' he declared fiercely, staring across the room at his nemesis, clenching his fists, ready to do battle. I pulled on his arm, turning him around to face me.

'You know the best way to get even with somebody who did you wrong?' I said.

'How?' he asked me.

'The next time he tells you something as stupid as this, you just look him in the eye and say, "That's what you think." Then you walk away.' Cashmere, one of the drag queens at the nameless bar, had taught me this technique, and I'd found it enormously effective.

'Just walk away,' he said, looking at me for confirmation.

'And don't look back,' I told him.

That was the first time he asked me if I was coming back again, but it was weeks before he would shake hands hello, and another month before he'd allow a hug; 'OK, but no kissing!' he said fiercely, holding himself stiffly as I put my arms around him. Still, I was making more progress with him than I was with the writer, who spent a fair amount of time soaking in the bathtub in his kitchen when he should have been writing or spending time with me. And once the three-month probation period had passed, Stevie proved to be a more reliable companion and a lot more fun. We'd go to movies at the St Mark's Theatre; he loved *Pinocchio* but cried when the boys turned into donkeys. We went for challah French toast at the Kiev Restaurant, and for chocolate-chip pancakes at Veselka. On Saturdays, I sometimes took him to the children's story hour at Books of Wonder in the West Village. The Bronx Zoo was too ambitious a trip, but we did go to the one in Central Park, where he rode the children's carousel and laughed hysterically at the snow monkeys, with their bright red faces and round white bellies.

'That one looks just like Sister Angela Rose!' he said, pointing to a portly primate, who actually did resemble the nun who was principal of Thorns of Christ Elementary School, where Stevie was in the first grade. Sometimes, even when the weather wasn't bad, we stayed at Thorny and I would help him with his schoolwork – or read him

Dr Seuss books and fairy tales from the skimpy library. He showed me the room he shared with three other children on the second floor, surprisingly large and cheerful, painted white and yellow, with posters of Mickey Mouse advising you to 'Read!' and pictures of other Disney characters covering the walls. There were two big bureaus in the room, and a large armchair against the wall by the window. 'This is pretty cool,' I said, looking around.

'It's very nice,' he said, in that solemn way of speaking he had at times. Then he looked at me expectantly. 'When can I come see your house?'

'Hmm,' I said. My apartment was a fairly large studio with a tiny study and a working fireplace. I had inherited it from a friend on the condition that I took care of JoMama, his golden retriever, while he was in Europe for a year. JoMama was a great dog and no trouble at all.

'I'll have to ask Sister if it's OK,' I told him. I had been about to spin a fantasy that included baking brownies, reading *Green Eggs and Ham* together and taking JoMama for a walk in Tompkins Square Park during daylight, when I remembered Sister K's constant admonishment: Don't make promises to the kids you weren't sure you could deliver. They'd had enough disappointments and already felt cheated by not having real families and other things that regular children had.

But it never came to that, because early on a Thursday morning in January, Sister K called to tell me that the boiler pipes in the basement had burst, the radiators were flooding the rooms, they were without heat, and was there any way I could take Stevie for a few days, until things were fixed? 'It's either that or I have to foster them out, which I'd rather not do for such a short time, it's so confusing for them,' she said.

I'm sure if I'd had time to think about it, I would have found reasons to say no; my work schedule, my drinking schedule, the writer who slept at my place occasionally since his was far more squalid, but right then all I could think about was Stevie shivering in his bed while the water ran over the floors. 'Sure,' I said, sitting up in bed. 'When should I come get him?'

'Now would be good,' she said, her voice harried.

When I arrived at Thorny, the kids were all gathered in the common room, and I recognized several other volunteers, all smiling sleepily. Stevie was standing in front of the bookcase, bundled into an oversized down jacket, a black watch cap pulled down around his ears, clutching a backpack. I knelt down in front of him.

'Sister said I was going to stay with you,' he said gravely.

'That's right,' I said. 'You're going to stay with me and JoMama for a few days, and –'

'Who's JoMama?' he asked suspiciously.

'JoMama's my dog,' I said.

'You have a dog?' he said, visibly brightening.

'Well, it's my friend's dog, but I'm taking care of him,' I said. 'Come on, it's freezing in here. Let's go home and make hot chocolate with whipped cream and marshmallows.' I stood up and put my hand out and, after a moment's hesitation, he took it and held on to it tightly.

I had already called work to rearrange my schedule and had visions of us going back to my place, drinking cocoa in front of a roaring fire, but it was not to be. There was paperwork; I had to go down to Varick Street to petition as temporary guardian. 'A pain in the ass, but it's got to be done,' Sister K said, handing me the papers. 'And sooner rather than later, I'd advise.'

At Varick Street, we went to a small office on the ninth floor with peeling walls and gated windows, where a clerk dripped ashes from her Benson & Hedges on to the petition, made copies and gave us oatmeal cookies and water. She leaned down from the height of her high heels and said to Stevie, 'OK, handsome, how about a kiss for a tired old lady?' He turned away and tugged my hand toward the door.

He was shivering with fatigue by the time we got to my apartment. JoMama met us at the door and began barking maniacally, pawing Stevie's coat, frantically licking his face. 'Sit!' I said sternly, worried he would frighten Stevie, but he just giggled and began scratching JoMama behind his ears. I fed him chicken-rice soup from the Chinese takeout on Second Avenue and gave him a hot bubble bath, which he found delightful, having never had one before. I filled the tub, agonizing over the temperature, the amount of water, so that it took twice as long as usual to get things right. What if I scalded him? What if he drowned? You hear about such things all the time, but you never think about them until you have a six-year-old sitting in your living room, waiting for the bath you promised him. I helped him wash his hair, which, to be honest, smelled a little funky at times, and then settled him on the couch with a small china cup filled with peppermint tea and honey, as JoMama lay on the floor at his feet, panting happily. He had his colour back and said he felt better, but I wanted to give him some baby Tylenol and buy milk and apple juice and graham crackers, kid food that I'd seen them serve at Thorny. I called the writer, who lived around the corner, but he wasn't home, so I asked Kyle, my upstairs neighbour, if he could stay with Stevie while I ran out for provisions.

I explained to Stevie, 'I want to get you some juice and food and medicine, so that you get a good night's sleep and tomorrow you'll be one hundred per cent. Kyle's a good friend of mine, and he loves to play checkers. I'll be back by the time you beat him at two games.'

'We'll see about that, mate,' Kyle said, winking. He spoke with a British accent, though he came from Whippany, New Jersey.

Stevie followed me to the door. 'You're coming back, right?'

'Well, of course,' I said. 'I live here, don't I?' Once outside, I hurried up the street so that I could return before he became too anxious.

At the corner of Second Avenue, I ran into the writer. He looked pale and preoccupied.

'Let's go get a drink,' he said.

I explained about Stevie, saying I had to get to Esteroff's Pharmacy before it closed.

'Hmm,' he said. That was his response when he wasn't really listening, when his mind was on his former lover, and suddenly I was tired to death of the whole situation.

'Look, I have to go,' I said. 'I don't have time for this. I have a sick kid at home. I don't have time for this!'

'Well, in that case, I'm going home to take a bath,' he said. 'I'll call you when –'

'Don't bother,' I said, turning to cross the street. 'Go home to your bathtub! Go live in your bathtub! Who needs you?' I felt fine and brave saying it there, in the street, and a group of young Latina girls gathered in front of the X-rated underwear store cheered me on. 'You *tell* that motherfucker!' they screamed, thrusting their fists in the air. I crossed the street against the light, with horns honking all around me. 'I have a sick kid at home,' I said to myself, and felt like a grown-up amid a sea of errant children.

It turned out that Thorny needed a whole new heating system. 'They're cheap and slow,' Sister K said, of the contractors hired to do the work. Stevie stayed with me for three weeks. He loved to help out, loved to push my antiquated carpet sweeper along the frayed oriental rug, do the laundry dance – a bit of play we devised while folding the laundry. I would put on my Motown records and we would dance around the room to 'Ain't No Mountain High Enough' and 'Chain of Fools', JoMama barking along with the music. He and JoMama adored each other; they spent the time between his bath and dinner rolling around on the floor together, and JoMama deserted me to spend each night sleeping at the foot of Stevie's bed. He loved the sky, loved walking home at dusk, when ribbons of colour fell into darkness, and loved it especially when the winter sunlight turned grey and gold on the horizon. One night, while walking JoMama and watching for shooting stars, which he'd read about but never seen, he pointed upward and said, 'Look! A rainbow around the moon!' And sure enough, the rings around the moon were tinged with colour. I told him to close his eyes and make a wish, which he did, and when he started to tell me what it was, I put my finger to his lips and said, 'Shh! Don't ever tell your wish to anyone or it won't come true,' and he nodded very seriously. We walked home in the moonlight, past the tired men sleeping in doorways and the snake people slithering in the shadows, whispering, 'Loose joints, loose joints, three for a deuce,' and when Stevie clutched my hand I'd tell him not to be afraid, they wouldn't hurt us and we were almost home, and he kept his small, mittened hand in mine even after we'd crossed First Avenue, right up until we walked through the apartment door. I felt a tiny thrill but I was taking things slow, and when I pulled the covers up around him at bedtime, I didn't bend down for a goodnight kiss, as he had not yet overcome his aversion to kissing. I didn't want him to pull back or turn away.

On the weekdays that I worked, I would run down to the school to pick him up at three o'clock and bring him over to the Yiddish Actors' Association for the rest of the day.

'Hoo-ha! Now a day-care centre I'm running,' Meyer shouted out the window. But he let Stevie look at magazines on the couch in his office and spent the late afternoon playing checkers with him, beating his brow and shouting, 'I'm ruined!' whenever he lost, which made Stevie giggle. Some nights he would take us all out to dinner at Sammy's Roumanian where Stevie loved watching the waiters squirt seltzer and drip chocolate sauce on the tablecloths while mixing the old-fashioned egg creams.

One wintry afternoon, as we were walking upstairs, we ran into Dixie, who was coming in to work, breathless and wearing a long red wig. I introduced them and she squatted down and smiled. 'Well, aren't you a little heartbreaker,' she said. Then she looked up at me and mouthed, 'Keep him,' before running up the stairs to the Pantheon Palace.

Of course I'd thought about it; how could I not? I even went downtown and got the paperwork to apply for fostering, thinking I could maybe adopt him down the line. But in the end I waffled; I wasn't ready, I didn't have enough money, and who knew what kind of mother I'd be? What if during a bad bout of PMS I threw him out of the window, or locked him in a closet, or any one of the horrible things that people do to children? And what if I met a man, a serious man, how would he feel about taking up with a woman whose kid wasn't her own? It was hard enough without that baggage. And then sometimes I'd think, maybe he'd be enough. On those nights when we'd have tickling contests, when I'd read him *Goodnight, Moon* as he curled up under the patchwork quilt I'd purchased at the consignment shop on Second Avenue, when he'd ruffle JoMama's fur and ask seriously, 'What's up, pup?', when I'd drink the one glass of white wine I allowed myself before going to bed, listening to his soft, even breathing as he slept in the next room. I'd think: maybe he's enough.

'Are you out of your fucking mind?' Ophelia asked. 'Yeah, sure, it's a nice little diversion now, but you have him around full-time – who's going to pay the babysitter, ever think of that? Or what, you're never gonna go out again until he's grown? You don't even have health insurance.' It was true; Isaac Bashevis Singer never did come to the phone, and Meyer had cancelled our Blue Cross the previous month. In the end, I told myself it was for Stevie, because I couldn't afford winter coats and summer camp, and he'd be better off at Thorny with a chance to be adopted by a real family, and part of that was true. But only part.

At the end of January, Sister K called to tell me they'd fixed the heating system and I could bring Stevie back the following Saturday.

'How's it been going?' she asked, though we'd spoken several times every week since he'd been staying with me.

'Great,' I said. 'Really great.'

'Well, I'm glad to hear it,' she said, something funny in her voice, but she hung up before I could ask anything. Stevie was silent when I told him, but later, on the way home from school, he threw his backpack on the ground and refused to pick it up.

'What's wrong?' I asked him. He stood there, arms folded across his chest, tears trembling on his lashes. It hadn't occurred to me that he would be upset about going back to Thorny; it was the only home he'd ever known. But then I remembered how he'd marvelled at having his own stash of chocolate-chip cookies, his own pork chop

GRANTA
THE MAGAZINE OF NEW WRITING

SUBSCRIPTION FORM FOR UK, EUROPE AND REST OF THE WORLD

Yes, I would like to take out a subscription to *Granta*.

GUARANTEE: If I am ever dissatisfied with my *Granta* subscription, I will simply notify you, and you will send me a complete refund or credit my credit card, as applicable, for all un-mailed issues.

YOUR DETAILS

MR / MISS / MRS / DR ....

NAME ....

ADDRESS ....

....

POSTCODE ....

EMAIL ....

☐ Please tick this box if you do not wish to receive special offers from *Granta*
☐ Please tick this box if you do not wish to receive offers from organizations selected by *Granta*

YOUR PAYMENT DETAILS

1) ☐ Pay £29.95 (saving £22) by Direct Debit
   To pay by Direct Debit please complete the mandate and return to the address shown below.

2) Pay by cheque or credit/debit card. Please complete below:

   1 year subscription: ☐ UK: £34.95   ☐ Europe: £39.95   ☐ Rest of World: £45.95

   3 year subscription: ☐ UK: £89.95   ☐ Europe: £99   ☐ Rest of World: £122

   I wish to pay by ☐ CHEQUE   ☐ CREDIT/DEBIT CARD
   Cheque enclosed for £ _____ made payable to *Granta*.

   Please charge £ _____ to my: ☐ Visa ☐ Mastercard ☐ Amex ☐ Switch/Maestro ☐ Issue No.
   Card No. ☐☐☐☐☐☐☐☐☐☐☐☐☐☐☐☐☐☐☐

   Valid from *(if applicable)* ☐☐☐☐   Expiry Date ☐☐☐☐
   Security No. ☐☐☐☐

SIGNATURE .... DATE ....

Instructions to your Bank or Building Society to pay by Direct Debit
BANK NAME ....
BANK ADDRESS ....
POSTCODE ....
ACCOUNT IN THE NAMES(S) OF: ....
SIGNED ....
DATE ....

⊙ DIRECT Debit

Instructions to your Bank or Building Society: Please pay Granta Publications direct debits from the account detailed on this instruction subject to the safeguards assured by the direct debit guarantee. I understand that this instruction may remain with Granta and, if so, details will be passed electronically to my bank/building society. Banks and building societies may not accept direct debit instructions from some types of account.

Bank/building society account number
☐☐☐☐☐☐☐☐

Sort Code
☐☐☐☐☐☐

Originator's Identification
9 1 3 1 3 3

Please mail this order form with payment instructions to:

Granta Publications
12 Addison Avenue
London, W11 4QR
Or call 0500 004 033
or visit GRANTA.COM

for dinner, without a bunch of other kids pulling and tearing and sharing his food. For days afterward, he raved about that pork chop to anyone who would listen.

'We'll still see each other like before, when I come to visit,' I said.

'It's not the same,' he said fiercely, through clenched teeth.

'No, it's not,' I agreed. 'But you know, at Thorny, you have your friends, and Sister K, and you have a better chance of finding a mom and dad, not just a friend like me.'

'Can't you marry Kyle so he can be my dad?' he asked, looking at me.

I laughed, then shook my head. 'Kyle doesn't like girls, remember?' I had explained this to him once when he asked if Kyle was my boyfriend, telling him that Kyle liked boys more than he liked girls. He nodded approvingly. 'I like boys more than girls, too, except for Lily,' he said, of the little girl who sat in front of him in school, whose long, golden hair fascinated him.

'I forgot,' he said now, dejectedly.

That night, I made him his favourite dinner of bow-tie pasta tossed with chicken and peas in butter sauce, with brownies and ice cream for dessert. Afterwards, he lolled around on the couch in his pyjamas.

'I feel a little sick,' he said, holding his stomach.

'Too sick to eat another brownie?' I asked him.

He looked at me, then sighed resignedly, sitting up. He put his arms around JoMama, burying his face in the dog's neck. 'No,' he said.

But he seemed fine when I dropped him off at Thorny the next morning. Before we left, I asked him to give me one little kiss good-bye, and he rolled his eyes, but pecked my cheek quickly, then turned and ran up the steps ahead of me.

I never saw him again.

The heating system was fine, but it turned out that one of the volunteers had molested one of the little girls, so this time they fostered out all the children, and I was surprised by the devastation that engulfed me when I heard the news.

'Buck up,' Sister K told me, when I showed up several days later for my weekly visit. She saw how quickly the tears came to my eyes. Her words made me angry.

'You could have called,' I told her, and then she turned on me.

'Oh, could I have?' she flared. 'We've lost the children, the diocese is talking about closing us down, the city may be suing us for child endangerment even though we screened you all and have everyone's fingerprints on file, but what was I supposed to do? I didn't want to put them in the system, I wanted to avoid –' She checked herself then, but I saw what was in her eyes.

'Do you know where he is?' I asked. She sighed, shaking her head. 'Well, can I try and find him? Where can I look?'

'You can try this number,' she said tiredly, writing something on a sticky note. I called and called and sometimes the phone just rang and rang and sometimes there was an answering machine and I left countless messages, but no one answered. I went down to Child Welfare and was sent to the second, then the fifth, then the seventeenth floor, which was vacant except for two desks and a filled-to-overflowing waste basket. I went to Social Services, and the woman there all but laughed in my face. 'Do you have any idea how many children we deal with in this office?' she asked, her lips curling in contempt.

I would have dreams that woke me in the middle of the night, my heart shaking inside my body. I dreamed that he was crying, wiping his arm across his eyes, saying, 'I tried to make friends, I asked them, "Anyone for a game of checkers?" But they just laughed at me and one of the big boys knocked the pieces all over.' I would sit up, smoking, unable to sleep for wondering where he was and what was happening to him. I kept calling the number Sister K had given me, I even went back to Varick Street, but the nice clerk wasn't there, and no one else could be bothered. I called Sister K, but she was embroiled in other phone calls and lawsuits and sounded stretched and exhausted, and she finally shouted, for God's sake, give it a rest, if I'd felt so strongly for the boy, why hadn't I tried to adopt him myself?

'There was no time,' I shouted back. 'One minute he was here, the next minute gone.'

'Well, there you go,' she said wearily, and hung up before I could say anything else.

One day, I burst into tears at work while collating copies.

'You maybe want to be an actress?' Meyer said nervously, handing me tissues. 'We got openings galore at the –'

'Shut up, old man,' Ophelia said. She came around the desk, took me by the hand, and led me downstairs to the bar with no name, where she ordered two shots of vodka.

'Sometimes the city swallows people, but that doesn't mean it's all bad,' she said. 'They're not all monsters, these foster people. For all you know, he's living with Ozzie and Harriet the Second, having a great time.' She raised her shot glass, which still had someone else's lipstick on the rim. 'To the kid,' she said.

It was Dixie's reaction, a few days later, that surprised me. We were on the roof, smoking; even though the wind was bitter cold, she was dressed in black fishnets and spike-heeled boots.

'Fuck you,' she flared, 'you fucking hypocrite.'

'What are you talking about?' I asked her.

'Everyone cries, once it's too late,' she said, grinding her cigarette to dust with her heel. 'When he's sucking dicks in the Hester Street playground, then you'll be happy.' She spun away in an angry huff, her heels clicking furiously. Things stayed bitter between us until she collapsed on the stairs from Aids-related pneumonia. The Yiddish Actors' Association disbanded due to lack of funds, and we were all forced to move forward and find our futures.

I stared at the picture in the newspaper. The article said he'd killed a man who wanted to pay him to have sex, then hanged himself in his cell at Rikers with his orange jumpsuit. He left a note that read, 'I got tired.' He was sixteen years old. In the newspaper photo, his eyes looked dead. I thought of him, in a strange bed, staring into an unfamiliar darkness, that tentative smile wiped from his face as the realization hit him that this was another kind of life than the one he'd been used to, that this now would be his life. For months I'd kept at it, calling those numbers, running to different agencies. Thorny had closed shortly after my last conversation with Sister K and was reborn a Howard Johnson's with rooms the size of a minute; Sister K had left the church, but I couldn't find her, either. And then gradually I stopped calling and running and went back to the rhythm of my life, thinking of him occasionally, hoping that because my own changed for the better, maybe everyone else's had, too.

I kept staring at the picture, searching his eyes. Wondering where I could bum another cigarette. ∎

SUMMER

Jacob Newberry

I met Jay two summers after Katrina, two years after my parents separated, two years after I came out. It was June in Mississippi: the palms sagged from the heat by mid-morning, their brown fronds shaking in the weak sea breeze. If you stood on the shore, you could see the barrier islands through the haze in the distance, small specks in an empty sea.

Jay was thirty but looked like a boy. He drove a black Jaguar with leather seats. It was his only indulgence other than travelling; his apartment was sparse, his walls unpainted. I had reconnected with Michael, one of my oldest friends, the year before. He introduced us. We were all old enough to drink but Michael and I were sometimes too poor, so Jay would buy our gin and we'd show him how to dance.

There were four of us. Jay was the oldest, but he looked the youngest. Daniel was tall and stunning, a dancer with black hair. Michael was a dancer too, but shorter. He had a sideways smile and dimples. I had black hair so long that most people mistook me for a girl. After a while I stopped correcting them.

We spent our weekends at the only gay bar within a hundred miles. It was on a backstreet in Biloxi, across from a fish market and Lee's Liquor Store. In Mississippi it's best not to advertise with a rainbow flag, and so the older patrons had asked the owner to take it down from the main entrance. *It's not safe*, they'd said. *We don't need to let them know where we are.* The owner had laughed and told them not to worry: *It's not the seventies any more.*

The bar had a patio out back, and the lights from the casino hotels shone brightly through the dark. The hotels were the largest structures in the state: they loomed over the water, shadows falling in every direction. They stood at every pole of the city, fluorescent bell towers marking north from south.

Down the street from the bar, the Hancock Bank was housed in a grey double-wide trailer on the corner. The old three-storey building had washed away in Katrina. Three wooden steps led up to the ATM, a small structure built into the wall of the trailer itself. A dark grey aluminium skirt around the bottom of the trailer kept raccoons and stray dogs from moving in below. If we found the right truck, we figured, we could hitch it up and steal the whole bank.

Jay rarely got drunk, but when he did he'd walk up to strangers and say things that made them hate and love him at the same time. *My mother has a top like that,* he'd say, *but you're thinner than her so it looks good.* We'd take him to the Waffle House up the road then, a pristine building that had reopened even before the casinos. Our favourite waitress was an old woman whose name tag read *Cricket.* We never believed it was her real name, but she was excited to see us every time. After going there every weekend for a month, she still thought I was a girl. *You gotta be careful hanging around all these men,* she warned me with a wink. *One of 'em's liable to bite.*

Jay wanted everything to be pink. His shirts were pink, his bathrobe was pink, his apron was pink, his soap was pink. He would add peppermint to his latte at Starbucks just so it would swirl into a light shade of coral. His favourite drink was a Sex on the Beach with extra cherries. The bartender named it in his honour, called it a Sex at My House because she knew Jay was too shy ever to order such a thing.

The bars were the first things rebuilt after Katrina. The unemployed and those in FEMA shelters needed a place to compare battle scars. *My whole house got torn down,* I'd hear. *That house had been in our family a hundred years.* Another would say:

My sister had to move to Houston. Last I heard she was sleeping in the Astrodome. The gay bar was flooded, but the structure was sound. After it was redone, the patio had a roof of corrugated tin, a cheap fix that never got upgraded.

One Friday night in late June a thunderstorm came in around midnight and we sat outside to hear the rain fall in heavy streams, the street light shedding an orange glow on us as we listened. A woman we didn't know sat on the patio near us and watched the rain fall. She wore a light blue jacket, though even with the rain and breeze the temperature was in the eighties. She took the last breath of her cigarette and flicked the butt into the parking lot. We watched as it fell, the slow sizzle audible above the falling rain, the last wisps of smoke rising weakly into the sodden air. *I used to love the rain so much,* she said.

We were all cast away from ourselves: the grace of the watering of the earth, the memory of the unrequited floods, the knowledge that for everything destroyed a new thing was created.

Jay loved Paula Deen. From her TV show he'd gotten the recipe to cook sausages in butter and stuff them with apples and Cheddar cheese. Her love of desserts filtered down to him, too: at The Cheesecake Factory in Atlanta he once paid for everyone to have a different flavour of cheesecake on the condition that he could try them all.

He told us one night, to our surprise, that he was out to almost no one. *You all are the first friends I've been honest with.* I told him: *I think everyone at the gay bar knows, too.* He looked concerned, then grinned. *Or maybe they just think I'm a good-looking friend?*

I'd never had gay friends. When I came out to my mother, she told me: *I'm still your mother, no matter what phase you're going through.* My friends at the time loved me, but I turned into an ornament. When one girl learned I was gay, her face lit up. She asked: *Will you help me decorate my place?* Guy friends started asking me for help with their hair. A girl I hadn't talked to since high school suggested we go shopping. One friend had me come by his place early before a date with his girlfriend. When we got back to his bedroom, he stood in front of the full-length mirror. *Which belt goes with these shoes?*

I told my father I was gay while we were eating ribs. He was taking a bite when I said: *Dad, you probably know already, but I'm gay.* He put the half-chewed rib back on his plate, slowly opened a wet napkin from its packaging and wiped his mouth and fingers, then looked at me. He said: *Are you sure?*

Jay was in the air force. He worked a support role in the military hospital. He'd been stationed in Mississippi after Katrina, since many of the medical staff on the coast had moved away after the storm, and for a time the on-base hospital was seeing any civilians who needed help. He'd volunteered to move, since the hospital was understaffed.

Most of the rentals in the area had been destroyed, so when Jay needed to find a place to live, he sweet-talked the older woman who owned one of the only remaining apartment complexes. *I'm just a young airman trying to help my country, ma'am.* He pointed out the rank on his uniform. *But it'll be hard for me to find a wife if I'm living on base.*

The bar was close to the base, and on weekends it would be packed with out-of-uniform military guys. One night the bartender came to us in a mild panic. *There's an air-force spotter here. He's taking names of all the people he recognizes.* The four of us fanned out, telling all of our friends quietly. Then Jay left in a hurry. Ten minutes later, the bar was half empty.

I asked Jay once what his parents would think if they found out he was gay. *I don't think they'd understand,* he said. *But I know they'd still love me.* His family was conservative and religious, just like all our families. He asked me if I had been scared to tell my parents and my siblings. *I was mostly annoyed,* I said. *All five of them in different states.*

I had to travel a lot that summer. It's not the sort of thing you mention in a text.

Michael and Daniel had both come out to their families years before. Their parents had come around reluctantly, first reacting angrily before settling into a cool, unspoken silence on the topic. My mother and I had reached the same state of détente: when I went to the gay bar, I only said that I was *going out*. If she was curious, some nights she'd ask: *Where are you all going? Maybe to a movie*, I'd speculate. *Or we might watch TV at Daniel's house.* In exchange for her wilful ignorance, I'd close my eyes when she prayed before our meals. I'd hold her hand and squeeze it when she said *Amen*.

In Mississippi this kind of treaty is a gift. I have friends who were disowned, friends who were beaten by their fathers, friends whose mothers said to them: *You'll burn in hell for this.* A treaty was the best Jay could hope for, but he wasn't ready yet to hope.

In July I ran into a friend I knew from my hometown. He had moved to Alabama for college and we'd failed to keep in touch. He'd since come out and was happy to see me. His mother had been one of the leaders of our church when we were growing up, and his father had been my Sunday-school teacher for a year. We had gone on the same youth retreats throughout middle school and the early years of high school, and his father was always a chaperone.

I asked my friend how his parents had taken his coming out. *They're angry*, he told me. He was a year younger than I was, and he had always been close to his mother. *She keeps saying I just need to find the right girl. I don't know, maybe she's right.* I asked: *Do you believe that? Do you still go to church with them?* He said: *I go to church every week. They'd stop giving me money if I didn't.*

A few months later, though, I heard through a mutual friend that he'd gone back in the closet. He'd been blackmailed financially by his parents into attending a camp aimed at using prayer and the Holy Spirit to overcome the 'temptations' of homosexuality. He'd been beaten down and faced with the prospect of being disowned. He'd caved.

I asked Jay again what his parents would think if they knew he was gay. *I really think they'd love me no matter what,* he said. *And they would never have sent me to straight camp. They love me, for God's sake.*

Jay's music collection was mostly contemporary Christian, a holdover from twenty-eight years of religion. I browsed through his CDs one night: Jennifer Knapp; Sandi Patti; Twila Paris. I asked him why he kept the *Wow Worship* CDs if he didn't believe. He said: *You never know what you'll want to listen to some days.*

Jay had been engaged to a girl named Karen before we knew him. They were college sweethearts. He proposed to her on the deck of a cruise ship. They were together five years before he told her he was gay. She said she didn't understand and asked him: *Do you still love me? Of course I do,* he said. *I always will.* When he was ready to come back, she told him, she'd be waiting. They stayed friends over the years, though they didn't talk much. She lived across the country.

Jay believed in old-fashioned romance. He had a crush on a boy who worked at the cookie shop in the mall. We teased him for loving eighteen-year-olds. *You should drive a school bus,* we said, *and then you'll get paid to pick them up.* We bought him a plastic yellow bus, wrapped in pink paper, and gave it to him at the bar. He held on to it all night, refusing to explain it to anyone who asked.

I lived with my mother during the summer. When I left for college, she'd moved from my hometown of Ocean Springs to nearby Gulfport. Our house was destroyed in Katrina, but her job as a nurse entitled her to expedited reconstruction. The house was small, but my room was there for me, every summer.

She had known Michael from when he and I were best friends in high school. By now I was working on an MA in French literature, and she met Jay and Daniel over the course of the summer. They'd pick me up for dinner and she'd insist they come in to see her. *Are you all hungry? I can make something if you want.* She admired my ability to find quality friends, no matter where I was. *You know I don't approve of your lifestyle choices,* she said, *but those friends of yours seem like pretty good guys.*

She took a particular shine to Jay. He smiled broadly and always called her *ma'am.* One Friday she insisted that I ask him to dinner, just the three of us. *His family lives so far away,* she said. *He needs a meal cooked by a mom.* I offered him some excuses, but he rejected them all: he was happy to come over.

When Jay told her that he'd volunteered to be transferred to Mississippi after the storm, she grew quiet. *That was a hard time to be here,* she said. *The doctors at my hospital told me to leave, they were telling all of us to get out of here. They said we'll all have cholera by the end of the month. But I stayed.* The only corners of our house not wiped out were her bedroom and my own, on opposite sides of the house. She lived in her bedroom alone those months, the late-summer heat turning the standing water in the living room into a series of mosquito nests. She thanked him for moving here, for diving in when the rest of the world was running away. Jay was silent. *But at least the MREs were good,* she said, brightening up. *The army was giving them out on every corner for three months. Have you ever had one?* Jay smiled. *Yes, ma'am. We ate them a lot in Basic Training. They were great.*

The next day my mother talked about Jay without ceasing. *Such a nice young man. So polite. What beautiful eyes. And he did the dishes!*

We stood at the counter, chopping mushrooms, Vivaldi playing in the background. She gathered up the vegetables and tossed them in the pan, adding pepper and garlic. I handed her the olive oil, changed the music to Prokofiev. *I love this piece,* she said, looking up. *What is it? It's his Third Piano Concerto,* I said, *my favourite.* She stirred the vegetables, their sizzling just audible above the music. *You really do have good taste,* she said. I nodded lightly. *But, then, you've always had good taste.* She went to the sink, turned on the water to wash the cutting board and the knives. *So what's Jay's story?* she asked. *Does he have a boyfriend?* She rinsed the dishes. I smiled. *Mom,* I said, *he's just a friend. I know he is,* she said. *But a mother wonders about these things.*

One night in early August the four of us stayed in to watch a movie at Daniel's place. After the movie was over, we decided to play Truth or Dare, minus the Dare. Each person could ask the group a question, and we all had to answer. My question seemed simple: *Who are you waiting for?*

Daniel said he wanted to sweep someone off his feet. Michael wanted to be swept off his feet. I said I just wanted the kind of nauseating romance that would make them all stop being my friends. Then it was Jay's turn. *I think I just want a family, to be settled, you know?* He glanced around at us. His eyes looked heavy. *I wish I could just skip the time between now and being settled.* Daniel disagreed, said that the fun part is the expectation. *Once you're settled,* he said, *there are no more surprises. Yes,* Jay said, *but it's so hard sometimes. I'm thirty now, and no one wants an old man.* We laughed at his foolishness, told him that thirty wasn't old and, besides, he looked nineteen. *Maybe so,* he said. *But I've wanted to be settled since I was nineteen. That's a long time to wait. It gets harder every year. You'll see.*

Summer ended and Michael and I moved back to our university town. We kept in touch with Jay and Daniel, but it wasn't until the following summer that we fell back into our old routines. I was finished with my graduate degree then, and Michael and I moved back to the coast so the four of us could relive the previous summer.

One day in July my mother mentioned that her pastor was starting a ministry for 'ex-gays'. He had been to a straight camp himself, and he claimed to have found both salvation and heterosexual desire in a four-week seminar. *He's really excited about what the Lord is doing for him,* she told me as she cleared books off the table. *I can't imagine what it takes to go through that.* I told her about my friend from high school, whom she'd known when I was young. *His parents forced him to go to one of those camps.*

She looked out the window, scanning the distance as if she expected some great vessel to approach the horizon. I looked out of the window, too. Our backyard was very large, and the fences had only recently been replaced. Our German shepherd had died shortly after the storm, so there had been no rush to fix them. She had left some of his old plastic toys in the yard, her small way of remembering him every day. I thought of him, the way he had been shuffled from house to house in the weeks after our place had been destroyed. In those early days there were no unbroken fences, only flooded fields behind flooded homes, a watery earth without borders. His nights were spent in cages, his days indoors with strangers, his few moments outside tied on ropes to trees. He only lasted a few months.

After a long silence, she asked: *Did it work? The straight camp?* I paused. The fence had been more expensive to replace than all the flooring in our house. It was new, guaranteed for fifteen years. The old borders of the earth had been replaced. There were no unbroken fields.

I guess, I said, my eyes still caught on the hard plastic toys. *I heard he's dating a girl.*

Near the end of that summer, Jay met someone. His name was Mark. He was nice, but the rest of us weren't sold. In the bar, he would walk away mid-conversation if he saw someone he knew. He never made eye contact. He would change the subject when we asked about his job. But he made Jay happy, so we told him we were glad.

Jay and Mark took us to Pensacola on a Saturday morning. Jay was being shipped off to Korea in a month, but he and Mark were going to stay together. I sat in the back, and we all sang, 'Where Do Broken Hearts Go' with the windows down. I sang out of the window to the old couple in the car next to us. The woman winked as the old man drove away. I saw Jay watching me in the mirror, smiling.

At the beach, Jay told us he didn't know how he'd get on without us. We should all come visit, he said. Of course we didn't have the money. *I can pay for your tickets.* We wouldn't let him, though we wanted to visit. Jay and I were the only ones with passports, anyway.

J ay was deployed to Korea and I moved to France to teach English. We Skyped sporadically. He lived in a three-bedroom house by himself and walked thirty minutes a day to get to Starbucks. *They don't know what peppermint is here*, he told me. He'd always had trouble making friends; away from us it seemed impossible. Mark could only visit every three months, or else Jay's commanders would get suspicious. He emailed me a few months later to say: *Mark and I broke up. He was cheating on me the whole time.*

The following summer I made it back to Mississippi. Jay made it back, too, but only for a week-long visit. He was being shipped to California now. I was there a few days before Jay got in, and he sent us all an email. *I know this is hard to understand*, he wrote. *But I'm getting back together with Karen. We're getting married in three weeks.* Jay said he was tired of waiting, tired of not having a family, that after thinking of the five years he'd been engaged to her, she was still the only woman he could imagine being with. *I'm still the same person you've known, and I still love you dearly.* Since Mark and Jay had broken up, Jay had been sick, losing weight. When he called up Karen, she told him she was raising a two-year-old by herself. Jay said he'd adopt the girl.

When Jay arrived he was distant and small. He had lost maybe thirty pounds. Before he'd left for Korea we had bought him a bracelet with all of our initials on the links. He'd worn it on his wrist every day during the week before he left. By now it could fit halfway up his forearm, but he wore it just the same, taking care that it never fell off his hand by accident.

At Daniel's house we had a drink before dinner. We stood in a small circle in the kitchen, ready to toast to the safe return of the one we loved. Daniel poured the last Martini for Jay, then set the shaker down on the counter. I waited for him to make a toast, but Jay jumped in first. *What did you all think of my email?* There was a pause in the room. *I just want you to be happy*, Daniel said, his eyes on his glass. *I'm sure Karen's a wonderful person.* Michael set his drink on the counter and hugged Jay. *I don't really understand, but I want you to be happy, too.* I stayed quiet. Jay searched for something to say. He seemed surprised. I stepped outside, saying, *I need to call my mom back before it gets too late.*

When the four of us went to dinner, Jay insisted that Mark come along, too. They'd stayed friends, despite everything. Jay texted at the table while we talked about the previous year. He didn't want cheesecake. He was wearing green.

As we walked to the car after dinner, he slowed down, motioned for me to wait with him. *What did you think of my email?* I said I didn't know. He pushed. *But what do you think of it, Jacob? Jay,* I said, *I love you a lot. I just really don't know what to say about it.* He hadn't seemed happy when the others gave their blessings. They were already at Daniel's car while Jay and I stood by the kerb in front of the restaurant. I avoided his eyes. It felt like mine was the only opinion that mattered to him. The sound of cars passing on the highway filled the air while he looked at me, then away. He wanted my blessing or he wanted my curse: but above everything he wanted to know that I loved him in a way that hadn't diminished. I scanned the sky for stars; it was a new moon, but the street lights blocked out everything above our heads. *Let's go,* I told him. *They're waiting on us.*

At the bar Jay wouldn't dance. *I'm engaged now.* He went to buy us drinks, saying: *I don't know when I'll see you all again.* I stepped out on the patio with the others while he was away. The offices behind the bar had been destroyed in the storm, and for years they had only bothered to pick up the debris. Now, four years after Katrina, the offices had been rebuilt, but the orange construction dumpster still sat in the parking lot, covering at least six spaces. The wind picked up as a thunderstorm rolled in. We waited for Jay, listening to the rain pooling in the dumpster behind the patio.

I asked the others if they had tried to talk him out of marrying Karen. No one had. Daniel said: *I wish I had the courage to marry a woman. At least he'll have a family now, be normal.* I was startled. I asked him: *You would marry a woman?* He took a cigarette out of his pack, cupped it in one hand as he brought the lighter to the tip with the other. *It'd just be easier,* he said, his voice small and hollow as he held in the first breath. Michael shook his head. *I don't understand any of this.* Daniel looked at him, shaking his finger in the air like he was scolding all of us. *There's nothing we can do about it now. They're getting married next week.* I looked at him sharply. *They're not married yet.*

Mark had been silent for most of dinner, and he hadn't spoken since we'd gotten to the bar. He wanted Jay back, but he knew it was too late. *He told me that he's sure this is what he has to do,* he said. *Well, he's wrong,* I countered. *Don't you think he's depressed?* Michael jumped in: *But how do we know it's not the right thing for him?* I slammed one hand down on the table, rattling the ashtray. It was harder than I'd intended, so I spoke softly. *How,* I said, *could this possibly be the right thing for him?* Daniel sighed, looked out at the water falling from the roof as he blew a cloud of smoke away from the table. *Look,* he said, *that little girl needs a father, and Jay wants a family. What's the point of fighting him on this?* Mark added weakly: *He's made up his mind. We're too late.* Michael hushed us all then, pointing to Jay opening the door with his foot, his hands full with drinks for all of us. *We have to stop,* he said. *He's coming.* Daniel whispered: *And we can't let him know we were talking about this.* I asked them, as Jay walked quickly through the door: *Is this what's waiting for us all?*

Jay walked to the table with our drinks. I thought of a morning two years before. Jay said: *Karen and I are going to Seattle for our honeymoon.* We'd all stayed the night at his place. *That's where the original Starbucks is, you know.* I woke up the next morning and Jay was making pancakes, a Paula Deen recipe. *Karen wanted it to be a surprise, but I pried it out of her.* I could see Jay's pink apron, tied around his waist. *They have a really famous fish market there, too.* He'd set out orange juice when we woke up, each glass a different colour. *They toss the fish like it's some kind of circus.* I'd told Jay it was too much, he didn't need to cook for us. *And of course we'll have to visit the Space Needle.* He told me a good hostess would never let her guests go hungry. *My dad said you can see the whole city from up there.* Jay had been humming Whitney while he cooked. *My mom says I need to get a digital camera before we go, though.* I'd sung the words with him. *Karen has a nice one but I want one of my own.* His voice was an octave below mine. *When are you all going to come visit me?* He'd smiled when I told him we'd never want to leave if he kept treating us so well.

Before we left I decided to talk to Jay. It was midnight, and the others were dancing. I found him inside, sitting at a corner table, texting his fiancée in the dark. I told him I needed to talk. He put his hand on my arm. *I've been waiting for you all night,* he said. *Karen's not even awake, anyway.* We stepped outside and walked on the sidewalk, the air filled with the scent of recent rain. *So why are you doing this?* I asked him. *I was hoping someone would ask me that,* he said. *None of them wanted to talk about it.*

The street lights shone down on the asphalt. There were no sounds except the vanishing bass from the dance floor and our own footsteps shuffling slowly toward the bay. The others, I figured, had forgotten our conversation already.

I think I just have to try it, he told me, his head turning toward mine. *I was so lonely after Mark and I broke up, and then when I talked to Karen, it just made sense, you know?* I said nothing, shuffling my feet noisily along the sidewalk while we walked. *She's really the only woman I could ever be with, I'm sure of that. We just had such a nice life together, and for so long. I really miss it.*

We stopped walking when we reached the overpass. We both turned to look out over the water. *Are you attracted to women?* I asked. *Are you bisexual?* He paused, looking toward the bridge. *I don't really know what labels mean,* he said. I insisted. *But if you had to choose.* He kicked a rock into the water, the small splash louder than the distant cars. *I'd say no,* he said.

So what is it, then, that you're trying? I asked. He turned to walk back to the bar. *I just can't do it any more,* he said. *I'm old. I'll never find a guy.* We walked slowly, deciding at each step if we should move on or stay still. *And besides . . .* he started, his voice trailing off. I looked at him questioningly. *And besides,* he said softly, *if this ends up being a mistake, it's something I'll learn from.*

It won't be just your mistake, Jay, I said. *There's Karen and her daughter now.* He nodded. *I know,* he said. I stopped walking and turned to face him. *And let's say the marriage lasts five years. If you think you're old now, how will it be better then?* Jay studied his shoes, then looked up at me. *Don't you think it's OK to just try something in life sometimes? To just dive in and sort the rest out later?*

I turned so we could head back to the water. We walked in silence, and I realized that I didn't know how to talk him out of this. We stopped when we reached the shore, standing in the same place as before. The bay glistened before us, the fluorescent reflections from the casino tower like some electric memory. I thought of the moment in *Long Day's Journey into Night* when Mary comes down the stairs with a wedding gown in her arms, her eyes glassy, her voice distant, saying to her family: *I'm always dreaming and forgetting.*

I spoke softly, my eyes focused on the distant support pillars that held the bridge upright. *I don't know what to say to you, Jay. It seems like you've made up your mind.* He was breathing quickly. *What you said is enough,* he said. I turned to him then, wondering if it was true. The night was overcast, the clouds coloured a deep shade of violet by the lights from the casinos. I took his wrist in my hand, looking for my initials on his bracelet. *I wear it every day,* he said.

Once, in the summer before he got married, Jay and I met the others for dinner. He picked me up. We were early, so we drove slowly on Highway 90, the road that winds alongside the beach for a hundred miles. He'd never known the coast before Katrina, and he asked me to tell him what was different.

In those days almost nothing had been rebuilt so close to the water. I asked him if we were in Gulfport or Biloxi. He looked at me like I was a stranger. *The way you'd know if you had passed into Biloxi,* I explained, *was when you saw the Olive Garden and the Red Lobster. But they're gone now.* There had been a fifteen-storey apartment complex nearby, but it, too, was gone. We drove along empty stretches of beach, sand covering paved spaces that might have been parking lots or the foundations of forgotten restaurants. *I think that was the Go-Kart place,* I said, struggling to remember. *And right next to it was the Cuco's where I had my first margarita.*

Jay didn't invite me to the wedding because he knew I wouldn't go. His fiancée had seen him only once in the previous three years, but she married him three weeks after he called. Daniel wrote on Jay's Facebook wall: *You have such a beautiful family now. I can't wait until I have one of my own.*

After Jay left, I talked again about his marriage with the others at the bar. It was variations on an old theme. Michael asked: *Why are you so upset about this? It's not like he's dead.* Daniel said: *You should be happy for him. He has something we'll never have.* I went to the counter alone, ordered a Sex at My House. I thought again of Mary, coming down the stairs: *I'm always dreaming and forgetting.*

When I first met Jay, when I'd just come out, when the four of us were together every day that summer, I told them once in tears: *I never thought I'd have the strength to live like this.* Jay hugged me, spoke to all of us. *Let's remember,* he said, *this is what we're living for.* ∎

New from BLACK CAT 😺

Blueprints of the Afterlife
a novel
Ryan Boudinot

'Take every high-voltage future shock you can imagine about life as it's shaping up in the twenty-first century, process it through one of the smartest and funniest and weirdly compassionate sensibilities you'll find on this crazy planet at this crazy moment, and you get a novel named *Blueprints of the Afterlife.* This guy Ryan Boudinot is the WikiLeaks of the zeitgeist."
—Robert Olen Butler, author of *A Small Hotel*

Me and You
a novel
Niccolò Ammaniti

"Immensely engaging . . . Both tender and emotionally arresting, Ammaniti's novel is unforgettable."
—*Publishers Weekly* (starred review)

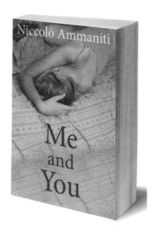

Beautiful Thing
Inside the Secret World of Bombay's Dance Bars
Sonia Faleiro

"A rare glimpse into dismissed lives. Faleiro brings a novelist's eye for detail and a depth of empathy to her work. A magnificent book of reportage that is also endowed with all the terror and beauty of art."
—Kiran Desai, author of *The Inheritance of Loss*

😺 **BLACK CAT**
an imprint of Grove/Atlantic, Inc.
Distributed by Publishers Group West

www.groveatlantic.com

THE
INTERROGATION

Vanessa Manko

DAY 1: JANUARY 19, 1920

Q. *What is your name in Russian?*
A. Ustin Voronkov.

Q. *Inasmuch as you do not believe in God, will you affirm to tell the truth?*
A. Yes.

Q. *What is your address?*
A. 116 Locust Street, Bridgeport, Connecticut.

Q. *How old are you?*
A. Twenty years old.

Q. *Where were you born?*
A. Province of Kherson, Alexandriyska, Ulesd, Bokas Volost, Village of Varvarovka.

Q. *Of what country are you now a subject or citizen?*
A. Russian subject.

Q. *Are you married or single?*
A. Married.

Q. *What is your wife's name?*
A. Julia.

Q. *Where is your wife now?*
A. She lives in Bridgeport on Locust Street.

Q. *Have you any children?*
A. No.

Q. *When were you married?*
A. There was no ceremony.

Q. *In other words you were never married to this woman religiously or civilly?*
A. There was no ceremony.

Q. *How long have you lived with this woman?*
A. About three and one-half years.

Q. *Why have you not married her according to the laws of this country?*
A. Because we live with her family.

Q. *Do you keep house?*
A. No.

Q. *How many rooms do you occupy?*
A. One.

Q. *One bed between you?*
A. I occupy one room by myself.

Q. *Does she sleep with you?*
A. No.

Q. *Why did you say that you were married?*
A. Because we gave an oath together.

Q. *And you state that you lived with her for about three and one-half years?*
A. Yes.

Q. *Where does she live?*
A. The same house as I live in.

Q. *Does she sleep in your room?*
A. No.

Q. *Did she ever sleep in your room?*
A. No.

Q. *Did you ever have sexual intercourse with her?*
A. Not officially.

Q. *How long have you lived in the United States?*
A. About six years.

Q. *When did you arrive in the United States?*
A. August 18, 1913.

Q. *Do you remember the name of the boat you came on?*
A. It was called *Trieste,* and came from Trieste to New York.

Q. *In what month?*
A. August, 1913.

Q. *Did you pay your passage?*
A. Yes.

Q. *Since your arrival in the United States have you ever taken any step to become a citizen of this country?*
A. I intended to take out papers, but I could not speak English.

Q. *Do you belong to any organizations?*
A. Russian Inspectors.

Q. *You mean that you are employed by the Russian Commission?*
A. Yes.

Q. *Where?*
A. In Bridgeport.

Q. *What factory?*
A. Remington Arms.

Q. *What was your occupation?*
A. An inspector.

Q. *Of what?*
A. Arms.

Q. *Did you have any preliminary work anywhere that fitted you for this position?*
A. I was a mechanic there.

Q. *Do you belong to any other organizations?*
A. No.

Q. *Ever belong to the Union of Russian Workers?*
A. I didn't belong.

Q. *There is such an organization as the Union of Russian Workers in Bridgeport?*
A. There was.

Q. *There still is?*
A. It seems they made it better, but the Union of Russian Workers has an automobile school in Bridgeport.

Q. *What is the name of the automobile school?*
A. The Russian Automobile school.

Q. *Was it known as the Soviet Automobile School?*
A. No.

Q. *We have information that this school was run and conducted under the auspices of the Union of Russian Workers. Did you know that?*
A. I don't know anything about this. I think the soviets started it an then the pupils took it over for themselves.

Q. *You mean the Union of Russian Workers started it?*
A. No. The soviets of Bridgeport.

Q. *What do you mean 'the soviets' of Bridgeport? We have no 'soviets' in this country.*
A. It was called 'soviet'.

Q. *Have you an automobile?*
A. No.

Q. *Did you ever have an automobile?*
A. No.

Q. *Why were you interested in automobiles?*
A. Because I was in the automobile business.

Q. *Were you financially interested in the automobile business?*
A. I am interested in every kind of knowledge.

DAY 2: JANUARY 20, 1920

Q. *Mr Voronkov, you have been to meetings of the Union of Russian Workers, haven't you?*
A. No. Only when they have lectures.

Q. *You have been to business meetings?*
A. No.

Q. *How many lectures did you attend?*
A. Two or three.

Q. *What did they talk about?*
A. About the origin of man.

Q. *They talked about the government?*
A. I cannot tell.

Q. *They never talked about revolution?*
A. I cannot know the subject.

Q. *Are you an advocate for revolution?*
A. I do not know.

Q. *You have no respect for the laws of man?*
A. I am a man. I have respect for them.

Q. *Why would you live with a woman three and a half years without marrying her if you had respect for the laws of man?*
A. We gave an oath together.

Q. *Are you an advocate of free love?*
A. Yes. We gave an oath.

Q. *You say you are an advocate of free love; that is not respect for the laws of man?*
A. I say, if we gave an oath – we will live together; get married.

Q. *You know about the laws in regards to marriage?*
A. Which ones? I would marry her by these laws at any time she demanded.

Q. *Are you an anarchist?*
A. No.

Q. *Are you opposed to the government of the United States?*
A. No.

Q. *Are your organizations opposed to any organized form of government?*
A. I am not opposed to government.

Q. *You don't believe in laws, do you?*
A. It depends on what kind of laws.

Q. *The laws of the United States.*
A. I've lived here six or seven years.

Q. *You didn't pay much attention to the laws though?*
A. If I didn't pay attention to the laws it would be a different thing.

Q. *What attention did you pay to the laws when you lived with a woman for three and one-half years without being married to her?*
A. We gave an oath.

Q. *What have you to show for it?*
A. I passed to her my property.

Q. *Is this 'oath' written anywhere?*
A. No.

Q. *Does this woman have anything to show that she has a claim on you?*
A. If she won't marry me, then I will see her corpse.

Q. *What is her name?*
A. Julia.

Q. *And you are here saying that she is your wife?*
A. Yes.

Q. *Have you anything against this country?*
A. No.

DAY 3: JANUARY 21, 1920

Q. *You understand, Mr Voronkov, this is a continuation of your hearing commenced on January 19th, 1920?*
A. Yes. I do.

Q. *Do you affirm at this time to continue to tell the truth?*
A. Yes, I do.

Q. *Are you an anarchist?*
A. No.

Q. *Are you a communist?*
A. I am not an anarchist neither am I a communist.

Q. *I show you a letter addressed to 116 Locust Street, Bridgeport, Conn., dated January 17th, 1920. Did you write this letter?*
A. Yes.

Q. *I will mark this letter together with translation of it Exhibit (1) and introduce it as evidence in your case. I show you another letter addressed to the same party. Did you write this letter?*

A. Yes, I did.

Q. *I will mark this letter together with a translation of it Exhibit (2) and introduce it as evidence in your case. There is a sentence in this letter that you have written to this young woman reading as follows: 'But there is possibility to come together although through difficult obstacles, so that we should care a fig for that dirty and stinking ceremony of marriage.'*

A. I wrote it. I was not feeling well. I was cross when I wrote it.

Q. *Then you were feeling cross because this young woman, when she found out that you'd be deported, refused to go back to Russia with you without being married?*

A. I offered to marry her in any way I could if I could get out of jail somehow.

Q. *It goes on to say in this letter: 'But there is nothing in the world stronger than love of heart and soul for only in it there is life and happiness, and not in that dirty marriage.'*

A. Yes, I wrote that. What about it?

Q. *It goes on to say: 'If you, yes, love me, as much as I love you, then you would spit upon all these disgustful calumnies.' Did you write that?*

A. Yes. I wrote that, alas. I wrote to my lover. I did not feel very well. I knew that our love was broken and in that condition I wrote it. I always offered her marriage, any kind of marriage she wants. You will find it in the letters that I offered her that. But she is my wife, you ask her. We gave an oath. She is my *zhena*.

Q. *Are you a member of the Union of Russian Workers of Bridgeport?*
A. I was formerly a member.

Q. *When were you a member?*
A. Four or five months ago?

Q. *When did you join?*
A. July 15th, 1919.

Q. *Are you still a member of the organization?*
A. No. I did not care for them. I quit.

Q. *When did you leave the organization?*
A. I stayed two months and then I left it.

Q. *On what points did you disagree with them?*
A. Because they hold on the same level workers and engineers, that is, skilled workers – this is why I gave it up.

Q. *The Union of Russian Workers is an anarchist organization, isn't it?*
A. I cannot tell you. I could not understand them.

Q. *A man of your intelligence certainly knew enough to read the basic principles of an organization before he joined it.*
A. I joined it because there were many Russians.

Q. *Don't you know or didn't you read the principles of what the organization stands for?*
A. No.

Q. *You know that if you are found guilty of the charges or part of the charges against you that you will be deported back to Russia?*
A. Yes, I do.

Q. *You said that you were a member of the Union of Russian Workers?*
A. Yes.

Q. *You stated also that you resigned as a member of the Union of Russian Workers?*
A. Yes, I did.

Q. *Can you tell me why?*
A. Yes. According to my convictions as I looked at it, I did not believe in their ideas.

Q. *Do you agree with government as it exists?*
A. No.

Q. *What is your opinion of the system of government you would like to see in existence?*
A. By name of science to obtain society.

Q. *Without government?*
A. Yes. Without government. People would be masters of themselves.

Q. *Without state?*
A. Yes. I believe it should be.

Q. *Supposing I would tell you that these views of yours are anarchist, would you then call yourself an anarchist?*
A. No. I do not consent to have any name, but if you want to call me that . . .

Q. *In other words you are frank in stating your opinion about society, but you do not know exactly the name for it?*
A. I cannot tell what the name would be but the form, if changed, would mean the liberation of the workers themselves by means of science and they will improve themselves and be masters of themselves.

Q. *Your views of society are that there ought to be no government, a stateless form of society?*

A. Yes. According to my opinion, yes. There must be no government or master who will say what must be done. Only science.

Q. *These views of yours could be called anarchistic.*

A. Well, my opinions are such. Let them call me an anarchist.

Q. *How would this condition of affairs without government, without state, be brought about?*

A. By means of science you can give your affairs to the people to govern themselves.

Q. *Do you believe in the use of force or violence to bring this about if necessary?*

A. No. I don't believe in force. Science is stronger than force.

Q. *Do you believe that the present form of government in the United States should be overthrown?*

A. Yes, very plainly, when the people will understand it can be done.

Q. *How will it be done?*

A. By means of science when the people will understand that they need no commander.

Q. *And no laws?*

A. I do not know how you can call them laws. They are just simply agreements.

Q. *You know we have people in the world whom we call anarchists.*

A. Yes, but I don't know what their ideas are.

Q. *They have views similar to these you have expressed here this afternoon.*

A. I said I did not know their programme, my opinions are just such.

Q. *Would you think it fair from your expressions or views here this afternoon for us to call you an anarchist?*

A. If you compare what I said with what you think anarchists are, then, OK, I consent to that.

Q. *I will ask you again. Are you an anarchist?*

A. It is so. I am an anarchist.

Q. *Have you anything further you wish to state at this time as to why you should not be deported in conformity with the law?*

A. I have nothing to say. Let them deport me. But let me take my wife.

They were married – officially – at Ellis Island. Two-sentence vows. He and Julia held hands solemnly. The justice of the peace read in a monotone voice, all the while smoking a cigar that created a cloud of milk white around them, an unfortunate fact that left him with residual memories of heavy tobacco and marriage. They would be leaving in one hour, two. He was taking her from everything she'd known and loved; she'd renounced her family, her country, she'd given up her US citizenship. It did not matter. Neither was willing to be separated.

The newspapers were calling it the Soviet Ark. The *New York Times*, January 1920, ran photos. The massive ship anchored at Ellis Island on a bitter day. They stood on the pier amid the wind and ice. The sky opaque, flurries like chipped ice. The only sounds the murmur of men's conversations, seagulls crying, the moan of the boat on the day's hard air. The anchor cranking like a scream; the massive chain lifted out of the ocean, iron-red rust, calcified with sea salt, seaweed. Just moments before, he'd sat on the long benches of the waiting room, the very room he'd sat in only years prior, eager to get beyond the bottle-glass windows whose light he knew was day in America – a country behind glass, the new country's light. Years later he would learn that there had been, in total, three other major raids

– the Palmer Raids. A series of round-ups of supposed anarchists or communists, men and women deemed a threat to the American way of life, men and women who might strike again – home-made bombs, subversive articles in newspapers, party meetings. They were plotting to take over the country. Somewhere, a man named Hoover had his name on an index card: Voronkov. Affirmed anarchist. Bail set at $10,000. Deported. ■

Station

The train station was a cemetery.
Drunk with spirits, another being entered.
I fanned gnats from my eyes to see into his face.
I saw father. I looked and shouted, 'Father!'
He did not budge, after thirteen years, neither snow nor train,
only a few letters, and twice on a cell
his hoarfrost accent crossed the Atlantic.
I poked his face, his mask slipped as a moment
in childhood, a gesture of smoke, pure departure.

Along freighted crowds the city punished,
I picked faces in the thick nest of morning's
hard light, they struck raw and stupid,
and in the dribble of night commuters,
phantoms, I have never found him. From the almond
trees' shadows I have looked, since a virus
disheartened the palms' blossoms and mother
shaved her head to a nut, gave me the sheaves
in her purse so he would remember her.

I was talking fast of her in one of my Cerberus
voices but he laughed shaking the scales
of froth on his coat. The station's cold cracked
back a hysterical congregation, echo and plunder,
his eyes flashed little obelisks that chased
the spirits out, and without them, wavering,
I saw nothing like me. Stranger, father, cackling
rat, I stood transfixed at the bottom of the station.
Who was I? Pure echo in the train's beam

arriving on its cold nerve of iron. Grave,
exact, the doors breathed open. Father was nowhere
when I boarded and looked through the glass
and plunged cold down the shadow chamber
many wore many strong disguises and none
spoke or even looked I was there in the box,
incandescent, becoming half their hush,
half still in the man's chiselling snarl, louder
now he was away and I am departing.

AMERICA

Chinelo Okparanta

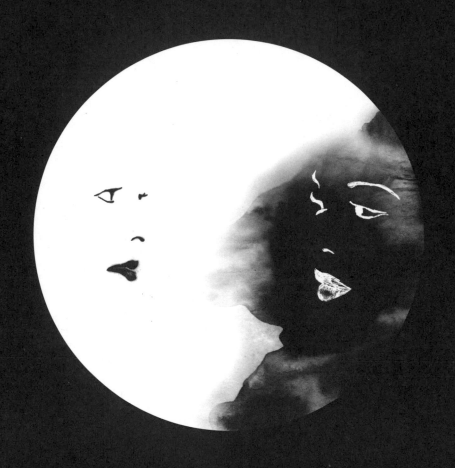

We drive through bushes. We pass the villages that rim our side of the Bonny River. There are hardly any trees in the area, and the shrubs are little more than stumps, thin and dusty, not verdant as they used to be. This, Mama has told me: that the vegetation around the Bonny River once thrived. That the trees grew tall, and from them sprang green leaves. And their flowers gave rise to fruit. Of course, this memory is hers, from a former reality, one too old to be my own.

The roads are sandy and brown, with open gutters, and with wrappers and cans and bottles strewn about. Collapsing cement shacks line the roadside in messy rows, like cartons that have long begun to decompose.

A short distance from us, something comes out of the river, a small boy or girl, maybe six or seven years old. Hands flail in the air and another child joins – typical children's play. Except that it's too early in the morning for that. Except that their skin, and even the cloth around their waists, gleams an almost solid black. That oily blackness of crude.

The bus moves slowly, and for a while, as we make our way out of Port Harcourt, I worry it will break down. The last time I made this trip (about year ago now), there was a problem with the engine. The bus only made it to the terminal in Warri, not quite halfway between Port Harcourt and Lagos. When we arrived at the terminal, the driver asked us to exit. He locked the door to the bus and went inside one of the offices in the terminal. He locked the office door too, leaving us passengers outside to fend for ourselves. We had passed no inns or motels on the way. Just splatters of small shops, their zinc roofs shining in the sun. Lots of green and yellowing grass. Clusters of trees.

At the terminal, I found a nice patch of ground on which I slept, using my luggage as a pillow under my head. Some passengers did the same. Others, I assume, wandered about the terminal through the night. The next morning another bus arrived. It took us from Warri to Lagos. I made it just in time for my interview. Lucky that I had left a day in advance. Not that leaving in advance made much difference anyway. As with the previous interview, my application was declined.

I sit on the bus again, slightly more hopeful about the engine and much more hopeful about the interview. I have not left a day early, but so long as the bus does not break down, I expect that this interview will be a success. This time I have a plan and, even if I hesitate to be as assured as Gloria is, there is a good chance that she is right, that very soon I will be on my way to her.

It was on a dry and hot day in November that Gloria and I met. The headmistress had arranged it all: I would be Gloria's escort. I would show her around the campus for the week.

That day, the headmistress stood by her desk, me at her side, waiting for this Gloria Oke. I was already one of the senior teachers at the time; I had been at the school for nearly ten years by then.

I'd expected that she'd come in like the big madam she was, 'big' as in well-to-do and well known, maybe with a fancy *buba* and *iro* in lace, with a headscarf and maybe even the *ipele* shawl. Even with the heat, the headmistress, and all the big madams who visited our campus, came dressed that way.

But Gloria entered, tall and lanky, a bit too thin to be identified as a 'big madam'. She wore a long beige gown, no fancy headscarf, no *ipele* hanging from her shoulder. Her hair was braided in thin strands and held together in a bun at the nape of her neck. Pale skin stuck out in contrast to dark brown eyes and hair. Her lips were natural, not lipstick red. On her feet, she wore a simple pair of black flats.

Even then, there were things I liked about her: the way her eyes seemed unsure, not being able to hold my gaze. The way she stuttered her name, as if unconvinced of her own existence in the world. And yet her voice was strong and firm, something of a paradox.

That first day, we spent our lunch break together, and for the rest of the week we did the same, me sharing my fried plantain with her, and she, her rice and stew with me.

She started to visit me at my flat after her week at the school was up. She'd stop by every other week or so, on the weekends when we could spend more than a few hours together. I'd make us dinner, *jollof* rice, beans and yams, maybe some *gari* and soup. We'd spend the evening chatting or just watching the news. Sometimes we'd walk around the neighbourhood and when we returned, she'd pack her things and leave.

I grew a big enough garden in my backyard. Tufts of pineapple leaves stuck out in spikes from the earth. They grew in neat rows. Plantain trees stood just behind the pineapple shoots. Behind the plantain trees, lining the wall leading up to the gate of the flat, an orange tree grew, and a guava tree, and a mango tree.

Once, while we stood plucking a ripe mango, Gloria asked me what it was like to teach science at the school. Did we conduct experiments or just study from a book? Were all of the students able to afford the books? It was a private school, she knew, but she suspected (quite accurately) that that didn't mean all the students were able to afford the texts.

I straightened up to face the wall that led up to the metal gate. Lizards were racing up and down. I told her that teaching was not my job of choice. That I'd much rather be doing something more hands-on, working directly with the earth, like in my garden. Maybe something to do with the environment, with aquatic ecology: running water-quality reports, performing stream classification, restoration, wetland determinations, delineations, design and monitoring. But there were none of those jobs during the time I did my job search, even though there should have been plenty of them, especially with the way things were going for the Niger Delta.

But even if the jobs had been available, I said, perhaps they would have been too dangerous for me, with all that bunkering going on, criminal gangs tapping the oil straight from the pipelines and transporting it abroad to be sold illegally. The rebel militias stealing the oil and refining it and selling it to help pay for their weapons. All those explosions from old oil rigs that had been left abandoned by Shell. Perhaps it would have been too dangerous a thing.

She was standing with her hands on her hips, showing surprise only with her eyes. I suppose it was understandable that she would have assumed I loved my job to have stayed those many years.

We became something – an item, Papa says – in February, months after Gloria's visit to the school. That evening, I was hunched over, sweeping my apartment with a broom, the native kind, made from the raw, dry stems of palm leaves, tied together at the thick end with a bamboo string. I imagine it's the kind of broom that Gloria no longer sees. It's the kind of broom we use here in Nigeria – the kind that Americans have probably never seen.

Gloria must have come in through the back door of the flat (she often did), through the kitchen and into the parlour. I was about to collect the dirt into the dustpan when she entered.

She brought with her a cake, a small one with white icing and spirals of silver and gold. On top of it was a white-striped candle, moulded in the shape of the number thirty-four. She set it on the coffee table in the parlour and carefully lit the wick.

I set the broom and dustpan down and straightened up. Gloria reached out to tuck back the strands of hair that had come loose from behind my ears. I'd barely blown out the flame when she dipped her finger into the cake's icing and took a taste of it. Then she dipped her finger into the icing again and held the clump out to me.

'Take,' she said, almost in a whisper, smiling her shyest sort of smile.

Just then, the phone began to ring: a soft, buzzing sound. We heard the ring but neither of us turned to answer, because even as it was ringing, I was kissing the icing off Gloria's finger. By the time the ringing was done, I was kissing it off her lips.

Mama still reminds me every once in a while that there are penalties in Nigeria for that sort of thing. And of course, she's right. I've read of them in the newspapers and have heard of them on the news. Still, sometimes I want to ask her to explain to me what she means by 'that sort of thing', as if it is something so terrible that it does not deserve a name, as if it is so unclean that it cannot be termed 'love'. But then I remember that evening and I cringe, because, of course, I know she can explain; she's seen it with her own eyes.

That evening, the phone rings, and if I had answered, it would have been Mama on the line. But instead, I remain with Gloria, allowing her to trace her fingers across my brows, allowing her to trace my lips with her own. My heart thumps in my chest and I feel the thumping of her heart. She runs her fingers down my belly, lifting my blouse slightly, hardly a lift at all. And then her hand is travelling lower, and I feel myself tightening and I feel the pounding all over me. Suddenly, Mama is calling my name, calling it loudly, so that I have to look up to see if I'm not just hearing things. We have made our way to the sofa and, from there, I see Mama shaking her head, telling me how the wind has blown and the bottom of the fowl has been exposed.

Mama stands where she is for just a moment longer, all the while she is looking at me with a sombre look in her eyes. 'So, this is why you won't take a husband?' she asks. It is an interesting thought, but not one I'd ever really considered. Left to myself, I would have said that I'd just not found the right man. But it's not that I'd ever been particularly interested in dating them anyway.

'A woman and a woman cannot bear children,' Mama says to me. 'That's not the way it works.' As she stomps out of the room, she says again, 'The wind has blown and the bottom of the fowl has been exposed.'

I lean my head on the glass window of the bus and I try to imagine how the interview will go. But every so often the bus hits a bump and it jolts me out of my thoughts.

There is a woman sitting to my right. Her scent is strong, somewhat like the scent of fish. She wears a headscarf, which she uses to wipe the beads of sweat that form on her face. Mama used to sweat like that. Sometimes she'd call me to bring her a cup of ice. She'd chew on the blocks of ice, one after the other, and then request another cup. It was the real curse of womanhood, she said. Young women thought the flow was the curse, little did they know the rest. The heart palpitations, the dizzy spells, the sweating that came with the cessation of the flow. That was the real curse, she said. Cramps were nothing in comparison.

The woman next to me wipes her sweat again. I catch a strong whiff of her putrid scent. She leans her head on the seat in front of her, and I ask her if everything is fine.

'The baby,' she says, lifting her head back up. She rubs her belly and mutters something under her breath.

'Congratulations,' I say. And after a few seconds I add, 'I'm sorry you're not feeling well.'

She tells me it comes with the territory. That it's been two years since she and her husband married, and he was starting to think there was some defect in her. 'So, actually,' she tells me, 'this is all cause for celebration.'

She turns to the seat on her right, where there are two black-and-white-striped polythene bags. She pats one of the bags and there is that strong putrid scent again. 'Stock fish', she says, 'and dried *egusi* and *ogbono* for soup.' She tells me that she's heading to Lagos, because that is where her in-laws live. There will be a ceremony for her there. And she is on her way to help with the preparations. Her husband is taking care of business in Port Harcourt, but he will be heading down soon, too, to join in celebrating the conception of their first child.

'Boy or girl?' I ask, feeling genuinely excited for her.

'We don't know yet,' she says. 'But either one will be a real blessing for my marriage,' she says. 'My husband has never been happier.'

I turn my head to look out the window, but then I feel her gaze on me. When I look back at her, she asks if I have a husband or children of my own.

I think of Mama and I think of Gloria. 'No husband, no children,' I say.

The day I confessed to him about Gloria, Papa said: 'When a goat and yam are kept together, either the goat takes a bite of the yam, bit by bit, or salivates for it. That is why when two adults are always seen together, it is no surprise when the seed is planted.'

I laughed and reminded him that there could be no seed planted with Gloria and me.

'No,' he said, reclining on his chair, holding the newspaper, which he was never reading, just always intending to read. 'There can be no seed.'

It had been Mama's idea that I tell him. He would talk some sense into me, she said. All this Gloria business was nonsense, she said. Woman was made for man. Besides, what good was it living a life in which you had to go around afraid of being caught? Mobile policemen were always looking for that sort of thing – men with men or women with women. And the penalties were harsh. Jail time, fines, stoning or flogging, depending on where in Nigeria you were caught. And you could be sure that it would make the news. Public humiliation. What kind of life was I expecting to have, always having to turn around to check if anyone was watching? 'Your Papa must know of it,' she said. 'He will talk some sense into you. You must tell him. If you don't, I will.'

But Papa took it better than Mama had hoped. Like her, he warned me of the dangers. But 'love is love', he said.

Mama began to cry then. 'Look at this skin,' she said, stretching out her arms to me. She grabbed my hand and placed it on her arm. 'Feel it,' she said. 'Do you know what it means?' she asked, not waiting for my response. 'I'm growing old,' she said. 'Won't you stop being stubborn and take a husband, give up that silly thing with that Gloria friend of yours, bear me a grandchild before I'm dead and gone?'

People have a way of allowing themselves to get lost in America,' Mama said when I told her that Gloria would be going. Did I remember Chinedu Okonkwo's daughter who went abroad to study medicine and never came back? I nodded. I did remember. And Obiageli Ojukwu's sister who married that button-nosed American and left with him so many years ago? Did I remember that she promised to come back home to raise her children? Now the children were grown, and still no sight of them. 'But it's a good thing in this case,' Mama said smugly. She was sitting on a stool in the veranda, fanning herself with a plantain leaf. Gloria and I had been together for two years by then, the two years since Mama walked in on us. In that time, Gloria had written many more articles on education policies, audacious criticisms of our government, suggesting more effective methods of standardizing the system, suggesting that those in control of government affairs needed to better educate themselves. More and more of her articles were being published in local and national newspapers, the *Tribune*, *Punch*, the *National Mirror* and such.

Universities all over the country began to invite her to give lectures on public policies and education strategy. Soon, she was getting invited to conferences and lectures abroad. And before long, she was offered that post in America, in that place where water formed a cold, feather-like substance called snow, which fell leisurely from the sky in winter. Pretty, like white lace.

'I thought her goal was to make Nigeria better, to improve Nigeria's education system,' Papa said.

'Of course,' Mama replied. 'But, like I said, America has a way of stealing our good ones from us. When America calls, they go. And more times than not, they stay.'

Papa shook his head. I rolled my eyes.

'Perhaps she's only leaving to escape scandal,' Mama said.

'What scandal?' I asked.

'You know. That thing between you two.'

'That thing is private, Mama,' I replied. 'It's between us two, as you say. And we work hard to keep it that way.'

'What do her parents say?' Mama asked.

'Nothing.' It was true. She'd have been a fool to let them know. They were quite unlike Mama and Papa. They went to church four days out of the week. They lived the words of the Bible as literally as they could. Not like Mama and Papa who were that rare sort of Nigerian Christian with a faint, shadowy type of respect for the Bible, the kind of faith that required no works. The kind of faith that amounted to no faith at all. They could barely quote a Bible verse.

'With a man and a woman, there would not be any need for so much privacy,' Mama said that day. 'Anyway, it all works out for the best.' She paused to wipe with her palms the sweat that was forming on her forehead. 'I'm not getting any younger,' she continued. 'And I even have the names picked out!'

'What names?' I asked.

'For a boy, Arinze. For a girl, Nkechi. Pretty names.'

'Mama!' I said, shaking my head at her.

'Perhaps now you'll be more inclined to take a husband,' she said. 'Why waste such lovely names?'

The first year she was gone, we spoke on the phone at least once every week. But the line was filled with static and there were empty spots in the reception, blank spaces into which our voices faded. I felt the distance then.

But Gloria continued to call and we took turns reconstructing the dropped bits of conversation, stubbornly reinserting them back into the line, stubbornly resisting the emptiness.

The end of that first year, she came back for a visit. She was still the same Gloria, but her skin had turned paler and she had put on just a bit of weight.

'You're turning white,' I teased.

'It's the magic of America,' she teased me back. And then she laughed. 'It's no magic at all,' she said. 'Just lack of sunlight. Lots of sitting at the desk, writing, and planning.'

It made sense. Perhaps she was right. But it was the general consensus in Port Harcourt (and I imagine in probably most of Nigeria as well) that things were better in America. I was convinced of it. I saw it in the way her voice was even softer than before. I saw it in the relaxed looks on the faces of the people in the pictures she brought. Pictures of beautiful landscapes, clean places, not littered at all with cans and wrappers like our roads. Snow, white and soft, like clouds having somehow descended on land. Pictures of huge department stores in which everything seemed to sparkle. Pictures in which cars and buildings shone, where even the skin of fruit glistened.

By the time her visit was over, we had decided that I would try to join her in America, that I would see about getting a visa. If not to be able to work there, then at least to study and earn an American degree. Because, though she intended eventually to come back to Nigeria, there was no telling how long she would end up staying in America. The best thing for now was that I try to join her there.

I think of Gloria as my head jerks back and forth against the window of the bus. I try to imagine her standing in a landscape like the one in the pictures she's sent. A lone woman surrounded by tall cedars and oaks. Even if it's only June, the ground in my imagination is covered with white snow, looking like a bed of bleached cotton balls. This is my favourite way to picture her in America.

I think back to my first interview. The way the man dismissed me even before I could answer why I wanted so badly to attain a visa for the USA. The second interview was not much different. That time, I was able to respond. And then the man told me how foolish I was for expecting that a job would be waiting for me in America. I held an African degree; was I unaware of this? Did I not know that I would not compare at all with all the other job applicants who would probably not be from an African country, whose degrees would certainly be valued more than any degree from Nigeria ever would?

I cried the whole bus ride home after that second interview. When I returned, I told Mama and Papa what I had done. It was the first time they were hearing about my plan to join Gloria in America. By that second interview, she had been gone over two years.

Papa was encouraging. He said not to give up. If it was an American degree I needed, then go ahead and apply to American schools so that I could have that American degree. It would be good for me to be in America, he said, a place where he imagined I could be free with the sort of love that I had for Gloria.

'It's not enough that I won't have a grandchild in all of this,' Mama said, after hearing what Papa had to say. 'Now I must deal with losing my only child, too.' There were tears in her eyes. And then she asked me to promise that I would not allow myself to get lost in America.

I shook my head and promised her that she'd not be losing me at all.

All the while, the woman I loved was there, worlds away. If I didn't make it that third time, I thought, there was a good chance she'd grow weary of waiting for me. If I were to be once more declined, she might move on and start loving somebody else. And who would I blame more for it? Her or me? All this I thought as I booked the third appointment. By then, I had already gained admission into one of the small colleges near where Gloria lived in America. All that remained was for me to be approved for the visa.

About a month before the third interview, Gloria called me to tell me the news. An oil rig had exploded. Thousands of barrels of crude were leaking out into the Gulf every day. Perhaps even hundreds of thousands, there was no telling for sure. She was watching it on the television. Arresting camera shots of something like black clouds forming in waters that would usually be clear and blue.

It was evening when she called, and mosquitoes were whistling about the parlour of my flat. They were landing on the curtains and on the tables and on the walls, making tiny shadows wherever they perched. And I thought how there were probably no mosquitoes where she was. Did mosquitoes even exist in America?

'A terrible spill in the Gulf,' she told me. 'Can you imagine?' I told her that I could not. It was the truth. America was nothing like Nigeria, after all. Here, roads were strewn with trash and it was rare that anyone cared to clean them up. Here, spills were expected. Because we were just Africans. What did Shell care? Here, the spills were happening on a weekly basis in the Niger Delta area. But a spill like that in America? I could honestly not imagine.

'It's unfortunate,' I said to Gloria.

'Something good must be made out of such an unfortunate event,' she said.

The bus picks up speed and I watch through the windows as we pass by the small villages in Warri. Then we are driving by signs for Sapele and for the Ologbo Game Reserve. The bus is quiet and the woman next to me is fast asleep, and I wonder how she can stand to sleep on such a bumpy ride. Hours later, we pass the signs for the Lekki Lagoon. We reach Lagos at about 2 p.m., an early arrival for which I'm very thankful, because it gives me plenty of time to make my way to the embassy on Victoria Island.

At 3 p.m., I arrive at Walter Carrington Crescent, the road on which the embassy is located. Inside the building, I wait in a small room with buzzing fluorescent lights. There is an oscillating floor fan in the corner, and a window is open, but the air is still muggy and stale. I think of Gloria and I imagine what she is doing. It is morning where she is in America, and perhaps she's already at her office at the university, jotting down notes at her desk, preparing lectures for her students, or perhaps even rehearsing for a public reading somewhere.

I imagine her in a gown, something simple and unpretentious, with her hair plaited in braids, the way it used to be. It's gathered into a bun at the nape of her neck, but there are loose strands dangling down her back. Just the way she was the first time I saw her.

I continue to wait. The fan oscillates and I follow its rotations with my eyes. I think of the spill and I remember Gloria's description:

something like black clouds forming in waters that would usually be clear and blue. The waters of the Niger Delta were once clear and blue. Now the children wade in the water and come out with Shell oil glowing on their skin.

I'm imagining stagnant waters painted black and brown with crude when finally someone calls my name. The voice is harsh and makes me think of gravel, of rock-strewn roads, the kinds filled with potholes the size of washbasins, the kind of potholes we see all over in Nigeria, the kind I imagine America does not have.

I answer the call with a smile plastered on my face. But all the while my heart is palpitating – rapid, irregular beats that only I can hear. They are loud and distracting, like raindrops on zinc.

The man who calls my name is old and grey-haired and wears suspenders over a yellow-white short-sleeved shirt. He doesn't smile at me, just turns quickly around and leads me down a narrow corridor. He stops at the door of a small room and makes a gesture with his hand, motioning me to enter. He does not follow me into the room, which is more an enclosed cubicle than a room; instead there is a clicking sound behind me. I turn around to see that the door has been shut.

In the room, another man sits on a swivel chair, the kind with thick padding and expensive grey-and-white cloth covering. He stands up as I walk towards him. His skin is tan, but a pale sort of tan. He says hello, and his words come out a little more smoothly than I am accustomed to, levelled and under-accentuated, as if his tongue has somehow flattened the words, as if it has somehow diluted them in his mouth. An American.

He wears a black suit with pinstripes, a dress shirt with the two top buttons undone, no tie; and he looks quite seriously at me. He reaches across the table, which is more like a counter, to shake my hand. He wears three rings, each on its own finger, excepting the index and the thumb. The stones in the rings sparkle as they reflect the light.

He offers me the metal stool across from him. When I am seated, he asks for my papers: identification documents; invitation letter; bank records.

'Miss Nnenna Etoniru,' he begins, pronouncing my name in his diluted sort of way. 'Tell me your occupation,' he says.

'Teacher,' I say.

'Place of employment,' he says, not quite a question.

'Federal Government Girls' College in Abuloma. I work there as a science teacher.'

'A decent job.'

I nod. 'Yes, it's a good enough job,' I say.

He lifts up my letter of invitation. The paper is thin and from the back I can see the swirls of Gloria's signature. 'Who is this Miss Gloria Oke?' he asks. 'Who is she to you?'

'A friend,' I say. And that answer is true.

'A friend?'

'A former co-worker, too.' I tell him that we met years ago at the Federal Government Girls' College in Abuloma. That we became friends when she was invited to help create a new curriculum. He can check the school records if he wishes, I say, confidently, of course, because that answer, too, is true.

Next question: proof of funding. I direct him to the bank statements, not surprisingly, from Gloria. He mumbles something under his breath. Then he looks up at me and mutters something about how lucky I am to have a friend like her. Not many people he knows are willing to fund their friends' education abroad, he says.

Then the big question. Why not just study here in Nigeria? There are plenty of Nigerian universities that offer a Master's in Environmental Engineering, he says. Why go all the way abroad to study what Nigerian universities offer here at home?

The question doesn't shock me, because I've anticipated and rehearsed it many more times than I can count in the month since that phone conversation with Gloria.

I begin by telling him of the oil spill in America. He seems to be unaware of it. I tell him that it has drawn some attention for Nigeria, for their plight with the issues of the Niger Delta. I tell him that going to America will allow me to learn first-hand the measures that the US government is taking in their attempt to deal with the aftermath of their spill. Because it's about time we Nigerians found ways to handle our own.

He doesn't question me as to how I expect to connect with the US government. He doesn't ask how exactly I expect to learn first-hand about their methods of dealing with that type of environmental disaster. Perhaps, having made a life for himself here in Nigeria, he, too, has begun to adopt the Nigerian mentality. Perhaps he, too, has begun to see the US the way most of us Nigerians do, as an abstraction, a sort of utopia, a place where you go for answers, a place that always has those answers waiting for you.

I tell him that decades ago, before the pipes began to burst (or maybe even before Shell came into the area – and of course, these days, it's hard to remember a time without Shell), Gio Creek, for example, was filled with tall, green mangroves. Birds flew and sang in the skies above the creek, and there were plenty of fish and crab and shrimp in the waters below. Now the mangroves are dead, and there is no birdsong at all. And, of course, there are no fish, no shrimp, and no crab to be caught. Instead, oil shoots up in the air, like a fountain of black water, and fishermen lament that rather than coming out of the water with fish, they are instead harvesting Shell oil on their bodies.

I tell him that the area has undergone what amounts to the American spill, only every year for fifty years. Oil pouring out every week, killing our land, our ecosystem. A resource that should make us rich, instead causing our people to suffer. 'It's the politics,' I say. 'But I'm no politician.' Instead, I tell him, I'd like to see if we can't at least construct efficient and effective mechanisms for cleaning up the damage that has been done. I tell him that Nigeria will benefit from sending out students to study and learn from the recent spill in the US, to learn methods of dealing with such a recurrent issue in our own Niger Delta.

He nods enthusiastically at me. He says what a shame it is that the Nigerian government can't get rid of all the corruption. He says how the government officials themselves are corrupt. 'Giving foreigners power over their own oil, pocketing for themselves the money that these foreigners pay for the oil.'

I look at him, in his fancy suit and rings. I wonder if he is not himself pocketing some of that oil money. But something good must be made out of such an unfortunate event. And of course I don't question the man in the suit about where the money for his rings and suit is coming from.

He fusses with the collar of his dress shirt and says, 'Sometimes when Nigerians go to America, they get their education and begin to think they are too cultured and sophisticated to come back home.' He pauses. Then, 'How do we know that you will?'

I think of Mama. 'I don't intend to get lost in America,' I say, more confidently than I feel. Because even as I say it, there is a part of me that is afraid that I will want to get lost in America. There is a part of me hoping that I will find that new life much less complicated, much more trouble-free than the one here. Still, I say it confidently, because saying it so might help me to keep Mama's fear from becoming a reality. Because I know that it might break Mama's heart if I were to break my promise to her. But mostly, I say it confidently because Gloria is on my mind, and if I am to be granted permission to go and be with her, then I must give the man the answer I know he wants: an emphatic vow that I will come back home.

He smiles and congratulates me as he hands me the green-coloured card. He takes my passport and tells me to come back in two days.

The sun is setting as I make my way down Walter Carrington Crescent. I look up. There are orange and purple streaks in the sky, but instead of thinking of those streaks, I find myself thinking of white snow, shiny metals reflecting the light of the sun. And I think of Gloria playing in the snow – like I imagine Americans do – lying in it, forming snow angels on the ground. I think of Papa suggesting that perhaps America would be the best place for me and my kind of love. I think of my work at the Federal Government Girls' College. In

America, after I have finished my studies, I'll finally be able to find the kind of job I want. I think how I can't wait to get on the plane.

I cross over to the next street. It is narrow, but there are big houses on each side of it, the kinds with metal gates, and fancy gatemen with uniforms and berets, and small sheds like mini-houses near the gates, sheds in which the gatemen stay.

I imagine the insides of the houses: leather couches and stainless-steel appliances imported from America; flat-screen televisions hanging in even the bathrooms, American-style.

But the road just in front of these houses, just outside the nice gates, is filled with potholes, large ones. And in the spaces between the houses, that corridor that forms where one gate ends and the next begins, there are piles of car tyres, planks of deteriorating wood, layered one on top of another. Shattered glass, empty barrels of oil, candy wrappers, food wrappers, old batteries, crumpled paper, empty soda cans.

I stop at the entrance of one of these corridors. Two chickens squirm about, zigzagging through the filth, jutting their necks back and forth, sniffing and pecking at the garbage, diffident pecks, as if afraid of poison.

I tell myself to continue walking, to ignore all of this foulness, just like the owners of the big houses have managed to do. Maybe it's even their garbage that saturates these alleyways, as if the houses themselves are all that matter, and the roads leading to them inconsequential.

But for me, it is a reluctant kind of disregard that stems from a feeling of shame: shame that all that trash should even exist there, shame that empty barrels should be there, between the fancy houses, littering the roads after the oil they once contained has been made to do its own share of littering.

Several streets down, I find a hotel, not one of the fancy ones, more just an inn. The room to which I am assigned smells musty and stale, and I can feel the dust on my skin.

I scratch my arms with the edges of the green-coloured card. I think of the possibilities, of the many ways in which I might profit from the card. I am still scratching and making plans for America when I drift into sleep.

The story should end there, but it doesn't. A person wishes for something so long that when it finally happens, she should be nothing but grateful. What sympathy can we have for someone who, after wanting something so badly for three long years, realizes, almost as soon as she's gotten it, that perhaps she's been wrong in wanting it all that time?

My second night at the inn, the night before I am to return to the embassy for my paperwork and passport, I think of Mama, her desire for a grandchild, and I think: Isn't it only natural that she'd want a grandchild? I think of the small children emerging from the waters of the Delta covered in black crude. Their playground destroyed by the oil war. And I think: Who's to say that this won't some day be the case even in America? It all starts small by small. And then it gets out of hand. And here I am running away from one disaster, only to find myself in a place that might soon also begin to fall apart.

There is a folk tale that Mama used to tell me when I was still in primary school. She'd tell it in the evenings when there was not much else to do, those evenings when NEPA had taken light away, and there was no telling when they'd return it. I'd sit on a bamboo mat, and she'd light a candle, allow its wax to drip on to the bottom of an empty can of evaporated milk, a naked can, without its paper coating. She'd stick the candle on the wax and allow it to harden in place. And then she'd begin the story.

In the dim candlelight, I'd observe the changes that took place on her face with each turn of her thought. Soft smiles turned to wrinkles in the forehead, then to distant, disturbed eyes, which then refocused, becoming clear again like a smoggy glass window whose condensation had been dispelled suddenly by a waft of air.

The folk tale was about an imprudent little boy, Nnamdi, whose wealthy father had been killed by a wicked old man who envied his wealth. Having killed Nnamdi's father, the wicked old man steals all of the family's possessions, so that Nnamdi and his mother are left with not even a small piece of land on which they can live. And so it is that they make their new home in the bush. There, they find a two-month-old goat kid, a stray, with a rope around its neck. Nnamdi's mother ties the goat to a tall *iroko* tree. Still, they continue to eat the green and purple leaves of the plants in the bushes for food, because Nnamdi's mother decides that they are to save the goat. It will grow, she says, and when it does she will sell it for so much money that they will be able to move out of the bush, or at least build a nice house for themselves there.

But one day, foolish Nnamdi leads the goat by its rope into the marketplace, and he sells it to a merchant who gives him a bagful of what the boy assumes is money. But when he returns to the bush, to his mother, Nnamdi opens the bag to find several handfuls of *udara* seeds, some still soggy, coated thinly with the flesh of the fruit.

His mother, angry at him not only for selling the goat, but also for doing so in exchange for mere seeds, furiously tosses them into the bush. The next morning, Nnamdi finds that a tall *udara* tree has grown, taller even than the *iroko*, so tall that its tips reach into the soft white clouds in the sky.

Nnamdi climbs the tree against his mother's wishes. In the uppermost branches, he finds a large, stately house-in-the-sky. He parts the branches, those thin stalks at the tip of the tree, and pushes through the rustling leaves. He arrives at an open window and enters the house that way. First he calls out to see if anyone is home. Once. Twice. There is no response.

There is a large table not far from the window. Nnamdi walks to the table. It is covered with a white cloth fringed with silk tassels. Nnamdi runs his fingers across the tassels. In the air, there is the scent of something savoury, a little curried, perhaps even a little sweet. Nnamdi follows the scent into the kitchen and there, on the stove, the lid of a large pot rattles as steam escapes from beneath. Nnamdi lifts the lid and breathes in the savoury scent. And then he sees it, through the doorway of the kitchen, in the parlour: a lustrous cage sitting atop a white cushion. The cushion is nearly as tall as he is. Inside the cage is a golden hen, perched on the top half of the hutch. All over the parlour floor, he sees coins, glistening like the cage. Glistening like the hen.

Nnamdi goes into the parlour. He climbs the cushion and takes out the hen. By one wall of the parlour, lined on the floor, are half a dozen small bags. Nnamdi peeks into them and sees that they are filled with more gold coins. He ties some of the bags around his waist, others he tucks to the hem of his shorts. He removes his shirt and makes a sack out of it. He slings the sack across his chest and carefully places the golden hen inside.

The wicked old man returns in time to see Nnamdi climbing down the *udara* tree. He pursues the boy, catching him by his shorts just as Nnamdi leaps from one branch to the next. The wicked old man gets hold of the bags of gold coins, but Nnamdi manages to wriggle away, escaping his grasp.

Nnamdi races off, gains ground, and finally lands safely in the bush. In fact, he gains so much ground that he is able to begin chopping down the *udara* tree before his pursuer has made it past the halfway point. Feeling the sudden swaying of the tree, the wicked old man scrambles back up to his home in the clouds before the tree falls. But he scrambles back without his golden hen, and with only the bags of coins.

The story always stopped there, and then I'd pester Mama to tell me more. 'What about the rest?' I'd ask. Did the hen continue to produce the gold coins? If so, for how much longer? And what did Nnamdi and his mother do with the coins? Did they build for themselves a huge mansion right there in the bush? Or, did Nnamdi give all the coins away like he did with the goat? Did he perhaps even give the hen itself away? Did they live happily ever after?

'There's no rest,' Mama would say. Or sometimes, 'The rest is up to you.'

That night, my final night in the inn, I sit on my bed and I recall every twist of that folk tale. I think of crude. And I think of gold. And I think of crude as gold. I imagine Nigeria – the land and its people – as the hens, the producers of the gold. And I think that even when all the gold is gone, there will always be the hens to produce more gold. But what happens when all the hens are gone, when they have either run away or have been destroyed? Then what?

The next day, I collect my paperwork from the embassy, and hours later, I head back to Port Harcourt to pack my bags. The bus bounces along the potholed roads, causing my head and heart to jolt this way and that. But I force my eyes shut as if shutting them tight will prevent me from changing my mind, as if shutting them tight will keep regret from making its way to me. ∎

THE ISLAND

Stacy Kranitz

Isle de Jean Charles is disappearing into the Gulf of Mexico.
Fewer than sixty water-damaged houses remain and more than
half of these are empty. In the past few years, the gravel that holds
the three-mile road leading to the island has slowly eroded into the
salt water, forming jagged edges that leave only one lane. The school
bus will no longer travel this road to pick up children. An onslaught
of recent storms and hurricanes has battered the island into a state
of deterioration. Ruined toys, appliances and mattresses from these
hurricanes line the streets. Dilapidated and abandoned homes
make for an apocalyptic landscape set against the beauty of the
surrounding marshland.

The island is now one-third the size it was when Native Americans
first settled there in 1876, fleeing south to avoid enslavement when
explorers first claimed the territory of Louisiana. The residents have
always made a living as shrimpers, oystermen, crabbers and trappers.
Today, there are fewer than fifty residents left on the island. Their
last names are Naquin, Dardar, Verdin, Chaisson or Billiot. Family
bloodlines run deep and often intertwine.

During the past five years that I have been visiting the island,
I have stayed with the Chaisson family: Hilton; his two wives Sue
and Judy; some of their twelve children; and so many grandchildren
I can't keep count. Their island is facing a bleak future, one that
reflects the United States' continuing neglect of native populations.
These images give a glimpse into the numerous rural communities
set along coastlines where water levels are slowly rising and residents
face a future compromised by industry, natural disasters and
government neglect. ∎

1. Angel, walking down Island Road during a tropical storm.

2. Dead fish line the side of the road as the high tide recedes.

3. Stephanie holds her baby during Mother's Day at the Chaisson residence.

4. Brianna plays with her dog along the bayou that runs through the island. The debris on the ground has accumulated after Hurricanes Katrina, Rita and Ike.

5. Fishing on Island Road.

6. Cody stands over a bird he killed with his shotgun.

7. Gage cries on the couch after his uncle Wilton playfully flicked his ear.

8. Two boys work to mend a chicken coop.

9. Caitlin hangs upside down in front of an oak tree dying from saltwater erosion.

10. A young boy plays using an abandoned mattress as a fort.

11. Nicole Dardar and her niece: 'If it was up to the government they would do away with the island. It may be washing away, but it's still home.'

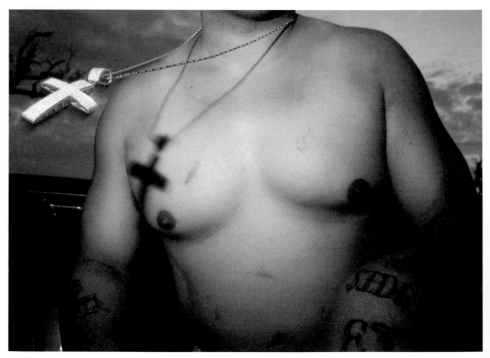

12. Nate.

13. Travis Dardar: 'When I was a kid they had trees all over. They had blackberries everywhere. If you look at the trees now, most of them are dead. They're still standing but they're dead. There is not one leaf on them.'

14. Mark Naquin sings Hank Williams.

15. Lonnie Dardar passed away just after Hurricane Ike severely damaged the home he built for his family.

16. Abandoned shrimp boats are nestled near the island's boat dock.

GRANTA

THE
PROVINCIALS

Daniel Alarcón

Calle Asunción. Huánico, Cajarmarca, Peru, 2001
Courtesy Daniel Alarcón

I'd been out of the Conservatory for about a year when my great-uncle Raúl died. We missed the funeral, but my father asked me to drive down the coast with him a few days later, to attend to some of the post mortem details. The house had to be closed up, signed over to a cousin. There were a few boxes to sift through as well, but no inheritance or anything like that.

I was working at the copy shop in the Old City, trying out for various plays, but my life was such that it wasn't hard to drop everything and go. Rocío wanted to come along, but I thought it'd be nice for me and my old man to travel together. We hadn't done that in a while. We left the following morning, a Thursday. A few hours south of the capital, the painted slums thinned, and our conversation did too, and we took in the desolate landscape with appreciative silence. Everything was dry: the silt-covered road, the dirty white sand dunes, somehow even the ocean. Every few kilometres there rose out of this moonscape a billboard for soda or beer or suntan lotion, its colours faded since the previous summer, edges unglued and flapping in the wind. This was years ago, before the beaches were transformed into private residences for the wealthy, before the ocean was fenced off and the highway pushed back, away from the land's edge. Back then, the coast survived in a state of neglect, and one might pass the occasional fishing village, or a filling station, or a rusting pyramid of oil drums stacked by the side of the road; a hitchhiker, perhaps a labourer, or a woman and her child strolling along the highway with no clear destination. But mostly you passed nothing at all. The monotonous landscape gave you a sense of peace, all the more because it came so soon after the city had ended.

We stopped for lunch at a beach town four hours south of the capital, just a few dozen houses built on either side of the highway, with a single restaurant serving only fried fish and soda. There was nothing remarkable about the place, except that after lunch we happened upon the last act of a public feud; two local men, who might've been brothers or cousins or best of friends, stood outside the restaurant, hands balled in tight fists, shouting at each other in front of a tipped-over moto-taxi. Its front wheel spun slowly, but did not stop. It was like a perpetual-motion machine. The passenger cage was covered with heavy orange plastic, and painted on the side was the word *Joselito*.

And I wondered: which of these two men is Joselito?

The name could've fit either of them. The more aggressive of the pair was short and squat, his face rigid with fury. His reddish eyes had narrowed to tiny slits. He threw wild punches and wasted vast amounts of energy, moving like a spinning top around his antagonist. His rival, both taller and wider, started off with a look of bemused wonder, almost embarrassment, but the longer the little one kept at it, the more his expression darkened, so that within minutes they and their moods were equally matched.

A boy of about eighteen stood next to me and my father. With crossed arms, he observed the proceedings as if it were a horse race on which he'd wagered a very small sum. He wore no shoes, and his feet were dusted with sand. Though it wasn't particularly warm, he'd been swimming. I ventured a question.

'Which one is Joselito?' I asked.

He looked at me like I was crazy. 'Don't you know?' he said in a low voice. 'Joselito's dead.'

I nodded, as if I'd known, as if I'd been testing him, but by then the name of the dead man was buzzing around the gathered circle of spectators, whispered from one man to the next, to a child then to his mother: *Joselito, Joselito*.

A chanting; a conjuring.

The two rivals continued, more furiously now, as if the mention of the dead man had animated them, or freed some brutal impulse within them. The smaller one landed a right hook to the bigger man's jaw, and this man staggered, but did not fall. The crowd *ooh*ed and *aah*ed, and it was only then that the two fighters realized they were being watched. I mean, they'd known it all along, of course they must have, but when the crowd reached a certain mass, the whispering a certain volume, then everything changed. It could not have been more staged if they'd been fighting in an amphitheatre, with an orchestra playing behind them. It was something I'd been working out myself, in my own craft: how the audience affects a performance, how differently we behave when we know we are being watched. True authenticity, I'd decided, required an absolute, nearly spiritual denial of the audience, or even of the possibility of being watched; but here, something true, something real, had quickly morphed into something fake. It happened instantaneously, on a sandy street in this anonymous town: we were no longer accidental observers of an argument, but the primary reason for its existence.

'This is for Joselito!' the little man shouted.

'No! *This* is for Joselito!' responded the other.

And so on.

Soon blood was drawn, lips swollen, eyes blackened. And still the wheel spun. My father and I watched with rising anxiety – someone might die! Why won't that wheel stop? – until, to our relief, a town elder rushed through the crowd and pushed the two men apart. He was frantic. He stood between them, arms spread like wings, a flat palm pressed to each man's chest as they leaned steadily into him.

This, too, was part of the act.

'Joselito's father,' said the barefoot young man. 'Just in time.'

We left and drove south for another hour before coming to a stretch of luxurious new asphalt, so smooth it felt like the car might be able to pilot itself. The tension washed away, and we were happy again, until we found ourselves trapped amid the thickening swarm of trucks headed to the border. We saw northbound traffic being inspected, drivers being shaken down, small-time smugglers dispossessed of their belongings. The soldiers were adolescent and smug. Everyone paid. We would too, when it was our turn to head back to the city. This was all new, my father said, and he gripped the wheel tightly and watched with mounting concern. Or was it anger? This corruption, the only kind of commerce that had thrived during the war, was also the only kind we could always count on. Why he found it so disconcerting, I couldn't figure. Nothing could have been more ordinary.

By nightfall we'd made it to my father's hometown. My great-uncle's old filling station stood at the top of the hill, under new ownership and doing brisk business now, though the truckers rarely ventured into the town proper. We eased the car on to the main street, a palm-lined boulevard that sloped down to the boardwalk, and left it a few blocks from the sea, walking until we reached the simple public square that overlooked the ocean. A larger palm tree, its trunk inscribed with the names and dates of young love, stood in the middle of this inelegant plaza. Every summer, the tree was optimistically engraved with new names and new dates, and then stood for the entire winter, untouched. I'd probably scratched a few names there myself, years before. On warm nights, when the town filled with families on vacation, the children brought out remote-control cars and guided these droning machines around the plaza, ramming them into each other or into the legs of adults, occasionally tipping them off the edge of the boardwalk and on to the beach below, and celebrating these calamities with cheerful hysteria.

My brother Francisco and I had spent entire summers like this, until the year he'd left for the US. These were some of my favourite memories.

But in the off season, there was no sign of these young families. No children. They'd all gone north, back to the city or further, so of course, the arrival of one of the town's wandering sons was both unexpected and welcome. My father and I moved through the plaza like rock stars, stopping at every bench to pay our respects, and from each of these aged men and women I heard the same thing. First:

brief, rote condolences on the death of Raúl (it seemed no one much cared for him); then, a smooth transition to the town's most cherished topic of discussion, the past. The talk was directed at me: *Your old man was so smart, so brilliant . . .*

My father nodded, politely accepting every compliment, not the least bit embarrassed by the attention. He'd carried the town's expectations on his shoulders for so many years they no longer weighed on him. I'd heard these stories all my life.

'This is my son,' he'd say. 'You remember Nelson?'

And one by one the old folks asked when I had come back from the United States.

'No, no,' I said. 'I'm the other son.'

Of course they got us confused, or perhaps simply forgot I existed. Their response, offered gently, hopefully: 'Oh, yes, the *other* son.' Then, leaning forward: 'So, when will you be leaving?'

It was late summer, but the vacation season had come to an early close, and already the weather had cooled. In the distance, you could hear the hum of trucks passing along the highway. The bent men and stooped women wore light jackets and shawls, and seemed not to notice the sound. It was as if they'd all taken the same cocktail of sedatives, content to cast their eyes towards the sea, the dark night, and stay this way for hours. Now they wanted to know when I'd be leaving.

I wanted to know, too.

'Soon,' I said.

'Soon,' my father repeated.

Even then I had my doubts, but I would keep believing this for another year or so.

'Wonderful,' responded the town. 'Just great.'

My father and I settled in for the night at my great-uncle's house. It had that stuffiness typical of shuttered spaces, of old people who live alone, made more acute by the damp ocean air. The spongy foam mattresses sagged and there were yellowing photographs everywhere – in dust-covered frames, in unruly stacks, or poking out of the books that lined the shelves of the living room. My father grabbed a handful and took them to the kitchen. He set the water to boil, flipping idly through the photographs and calling out names of the relatives in each picture as he passed them along. There was a flatness to his voice, a distance – as if he were testing his recall, as opposed to reliving any cherished childhood memory. You got the sense he barely knew these people.

He handed me a small black-and-white image with a matt finish, printed on heavy card stock with scalloped edges. It was a group shot taken in front of this very house, back when it was surrounded by fallow land, the bare, undeveloped hillside. Perhaps twenty blurred faces.

'Besides a few of the babies,' my father said, 'everyone else in this photo is dead.'

For a while we didn't speak.

A bloom of mould grew wild on the kitchen wall, bursting black and menacing from a crack in the cement. To pass the time, or change the subject, we considered the mould's shape, evocative of something, but we couldn't say what. A baby carriage? A bull?

'Joselito's moto-taxi,' my father said.

And this was, in fact, exactly what it resembled.

'May he rest in peace,' I added.

My father had been quiet for most of the trip – coming home always did this to him – but he spoke up now. Joselito, he said, must have been a real character. Someone special. He hadn't seen an outpouring of emotion like that in many years, not since he was a boy.

'It was an act,' I said, and began to explain my theory.

My old man interrupted me. 'But what isn't?'

What he meant was that people perform sorrow for a reason. For example: no one was performing it for Raúl. My great-uncle had been mayor of this town when my father was a boy, had owned the filling station, and sired seven children with five different women, none of whom he bothered to marry. He'd run the town's only radio station for a decade, and paid from his own pocket to pave the main boulevard, so he could drive in style. Then in the late 1980s, Raúl lost most of his money, and settled into a bitter seclusion. I remembered him only for his bulbous nose and his hatred of foreigners, an expansive category in which he placed anyone who wasn't originally from the town and its surrounding areas. Raúl's distrust of the capital was absolute. I was eleven the last time I saw him, and I don't think he ever eyed me with anything but suspicion.

It was easier to talk about Joselito than about my great-uncle. More pleasant perhaps. This town brought up bad memories for my father, who was, in those days, entering a pensive late-middle age. That was how it seemed to me at the time, but what does a twenty-two-year-old know about a grown man's life and worries? I was too young to recognize what would later seem more than obvious: that I was the greatest source of my old man's concern. That if he were growing old too soon, I was at least partly to blame. This would've been clear, had I been paying attention.

My father shifted the conversation. He brought the tea out, and asked me what I planned to do when I got to California. This was typical of the time, a speculative game we were fond of playing. We assumed it was fast approaching, the date of my departure; later, I would think we'd all been pretending.

'I don't know,' I said.

I'd spent so much time imagining it – my leaving, my preparations, my victory lap around the city, saying goodbye and good luck to all those who'd be staying behind – but what came after contained few specifics. I'd get off the plane, and then . . . Francisco, I guess, would be there. He'd drive me across the Bay Bridge to Oakland, and introduce me to his life there, whatever that might be. From time to time, when curiosity seized me, I searched for this place online and found news items that helped me begin to envision it: shootings mostly, but also minor political scandals involving graft or misused patronage or a city official with liens on his property; occasionally something really exciting, like an oil tanker lost in fog and hitting a bridge, or the firebombing of a liquor store by one street gang or another. There'd even been a minor riot not too long before, with the requisite smashed windows, a dumpster in flames, and a set of multiracial anarchists wearing bandannas across their faces so that all you could see in the photos were their alert and feral eyes; and I'd wondered then how my brother had chosen to live in a city whose ambience so closely mimicked our own. Could it really be an accident of geography? Or was it some latent homing instinct?

What it all had to do with me was never quite clear. Where I would fit in. What I would do with myself once I was there. These were among the many questions that remained. The visa, whenever it came, would not arrive with life instructions. Nor would it obligate me to stay in Oakland, of course, and I had considered other alternatives, though none very seriously, and all based on a whimsical set of readings and the occasional Internet search: Philadelphia, I liked for its history; Miami, for its tropical ennui; Chicago, for its poets; Los Angeles, for its sheer size.

But one can start over any number of places, right? Any number of times?

'I'll get a job,' I told my father. 'Isn't that what Americans do?'

'It's what everyone does. In a copy shop?'

'I'm an actor.'

'Who makes photocopies.'

I frowned. 'So I'll make photocopies my entire life. Why not?'

He wanted me to study, because that was what he'd wanted for himself so many years before. And for Francisco, too. He'd hoped my brother would be a professor by now, an academic, though he was far too proud ever to share this disappointment with me. He had his own issues with me: his unbounded respect for playwrights and artists and writers was completely abstract; on a more concrete level, he wished I'd considered some more reliable way to earn a living. As for my day job, my mother told me once that seeing me work as the attendant at the copy shop made my old man sad. His sadness, in turn, made me angry. His politics affirmed that all work held an inherent dignity. This was what he'd always repeated, but of course no ideology can protect a son from the unwelcome inheritance of his father's ambitions.

'When I was a boy,' my old man said, 'this town was the middle of nowhere. It still is, I know. But imagine it before they re-routed the highway. We knew there was something else out there – another country to the south, the capital to the north – but it felt very far away.'

'It was.'

'You're right. It was. We were hours from civilization. Six or seven to the border, if not more. But the roads were awful. And *spiritually* – it was even further. It required a certain kind of imagination to see it.'

I smiled. I thought I was making him laugh, but really I was just trying to close off the conversation, shut it down before it headed somewhere I didn't want it to go. 'I've always been very imaginative,' I said.

My old man knew what I was doing, even if I didn't.

'Yes, son. You have. Maybe not imaginative enough, though.'

I didn't want to ask him what he meant, so I sat, letting it linger until the silence forced him to answer my unspoken question.

'I'm sorry,' my old man said. 'I wonder if you've thought much about your future, that's all.'

'Sure I have. All the time.'

'To the exclusion of thinking about your present?'

'I wouldn't say that.'

'What would you say?'

I paused, attempting to strip my voice of any anger before I spoke. 'I've thought a great deal about my future, so that my present could seem more liveable.'

He nodded slowly. We sipped carefully from our steaming cups. For once, I was grateful for my old man's obsession with tea – it allowed us to pause, gather our thoughts. It excused us from having to talk, and the danger of saying things we might not mean.

'You and Rocío seem well.'

I never spoke about my relationships with my parents.

'Sure. We're doing fine.'

There was something else he wanted to ask me, I could tell, but he didn't. He narrowed his eyes, thinking, and then something changed in his face – a slackness emerged, the edges of his mouth dropped. He'd given up.

'I always hated this house,' my old man said after a few minutes. 'I can't imagine that anyone would want it. We should bulldoze the thing and be done with it.'

It was all the same to me, and I told him so. We could set it on fire, or shatter every last brick with a sledgehammer. I had no attachments to this place, to this town. My father did, but he preferred not to think about them. It was a place to visit with a heavy heart, when an old relative died. Or with your family on holiday, if such a luxury could be afforded. Francisco, it occurred to me, might feel the same way towards the city where we'd been raised.

'I've let you down,' my old man said. His voice was timid, hushed, as if he hadn't wanted me to hear.

'Don't say that.'

'We should have pushed you harder, sent you away sooner. Now . . . ' He didn't finish, but I understood that *now*, in his estimation, was far too late.

'It's fine.'

'I know it is. Everyone's fine. I'm fine, you're fine, your mother's fine, too. Even Francisco is fine, or so the rumour goes, God bless the USA. Everything is fine. Just ask the mummies sitting on the benches out there. They spend every evening telling the same five stories again and again, but if you ask them, they'll respond with a single voice that everything is *just fine*. What do we have to complain about?'

'I'm not complaining,' I said.

'I know you aren't. That's precisely what concerns me.'

I slumped, feeling deflated. 'I'll leave when the visa comes. I can't leave before that. I can't do anything before that.'

My father winced. 'But it isn't entirely accurate to say you can't do *anything*, is it?'

'I suppose not.'

'Consider this: what if it doesn't come? Or what if it comes at an inconvenient time. Let's say you're in love with Rocío –'

'Let's suppose.'

'And she doesn't want to leave. So then you stay. What will you do then?'

He was really asking: *What are you doing right now?*

When I didn't say anything, he pressed further, his voice rising in pitch. 'Tell me, son. Are you sure you even want that visa? Are you absolutely certain? Do you know yet what you're going to do with your life?'

We were determined not to shout at each other. Eventually, he went to bed, and I left the house for a walk along the town's desolate streets, where there was not a car to be seen, nor a person. You could hear the occasional truck roaring by in the distance, but fewer at this hour, like a sporadic wind. It looked like an abandoned stage set, and I wondered: who's *absolutely certain* about anything? I found a payphone not far from the plaza, and called Rocío. I wanted her to make me laugh, and I sighed with relief when she answered on the first ring, as if she'd been waiting for my call. Maybe she had. I told her about the drive, about the fight we witnessed, about my great-uncle's dank and oppressive house, filled with pictures of racehorses and marching bands and the various women who'd borne his children and had their hopes and their hearts shattered. I didn't tell her about the conversation with my father.

'I've taken a lover,' Rocío said, interrupting.

It was a game we played; I tried to muster the energy to play along. I didn't want to disappoint her. 'And what's he like?'

'Handsome, in an ugly sort of way. Crooked nose, giant cock. More than adequate.'

'I'm dying of jealousy,' I said. 'Literally dying. The life seeps from my tired body.'

'Did you know that by law, if a man finds his wife sleeping with another man on their marriage bed, he's allowed to murder them both?'

'I hadn't heard that. But what if he finds them on the couch?'

'Then he can't kill them. Legally speaking.'

'So did you sleep with him on our bed?'

'Yes,' Rocío answered. 'Many, many times.'

'And was his name Joselito?'

There was quiet. 'Yes. That was his name.'

'I've already had him killed.'

'But I just saw him this morning.'

'He's gone, baby. Say goodbye.'

'Goodbye,' she whispered.

I was satisfied with myself. She asked me about the town, and I told her that everyone confused me with my brother. So many years separated my family from this place that they'd simply lost track of me. There was room in their heads for only one son; was it any surprise they chose Francisco?

'Oh, that's so sad!' Rocío said. She was mocking me.

'I'm not telling you so you'll feel sorry for me.'

'Of course not.'

'I'm serious.'

'I know,' she said, drawing the syllable out in a way she probably thought was cute, but which just annoyed me.

'I'm hanging up now.' The phonecard was running out anyway.

'Goodnight, Joselito,' Rocío said, and blew a kiss into the receiver.

We spent a few hours the next morning in my great-uncle's house, sifting through the clutter, in case there were anything we might want to take back with us. There wasn't. My father set some items aside for the soldiers, should it come to that; nothing very expensive, but things he thought might *look* expensive if you were a bored young man with a rifle who'd missed all the action by a few years, and were serving your time standing by the side of a highway, collecting tributes: a silver picture frame; an antique camera in pristine condition; an old but very ornate trophy, which would surely come back to life with a little polish. It didn't make much sense, of course; these young men wanted one of two things, I told my father: cash or electronics. Sex, perhaps, but probably not with us. Anything else was meaningless. My father agreed.

Our unfinished conversation was not mentioned.

After lunch, we headed into town. There was some paperwork to be filed in order to transfer Raúl's property over to a distant cousin of ours, an unmarried woman of fifty who still lived nearby and might have some use for the house. Raúl's children wanted nothing, refused, on principle, to be involved. My father was dreading this transfer, of course, not because he was reluctant to give up the property, but because he was afraid of how many hours this relatively simple bureaucratic chore might require. But he hadn't taken his local celebrity into account, and of course we were received at city records with the same bright and enthusiastic palaver with which we'd been welcomed in the plaza the night before. We were taken around to greet each of the dozen municipal employees, friendly men and women of my father's generation and older who welcomed the interruption because they quite clearly had nothing to do. It was just like evenings in the plaza, I thought, only behind desks and under fluorescent lights. Many of them claimed some vague familial connection to me, especially the older ones, and so I began calling them all *uncle* and *auntie* just to be safe. Again and again I was mistaken for Francisco – When did you get back? Where are you living now? – and I began to respond with increasingly imprecise answers, so that finally, when we'd made it inside the last office, the registrar of properties, I simply gave in to this assumption, and said, when asked: 'I live in California.'

It felt good to say it. A relief.

The registrar was a small, very round man named Juan, with dark skin and a raspy voice. He'd been my father's best friend in third grade, or so he claimed. My old man didn't bother to contradict him, only smiled in such a way that I understood it to be untrue; or if not untrue exactly, then one of those statements that time had rendered unverifiable, and about which there was no longer any use debating.

The registrar liked my answer. He loosened his tie and clapped his hands. 'California! Oh, my! So what do you do there?'

My father gave me a once-over. 'Yes,' he said now. 'Tell my old friend Juan what you do.'

I thought back to all those letters my brother had written, all those stories of his I'd read and nearly memorized in my adolescence. It didn't matter, of course; I could have told Juan any number of things: about my work as a ski instructor, or as a baggage handler, or as a bike-repair technician. I could have told him the ins and outs of Wal-Mart, about life in American small towns, about the shifting customs and mores of different regions of the vast United States. The accents, the landscapes, the winters. Anything I said at that moment would've worked just fine. But I went with something simple and current, guessing correctly that Juan wasn't much interested in details. There were a few facts I knew about my brother, in spite of the years and the distance: a man named Hassan had taken him under his wing. They were in business together, selling baby formula and low-priced denim and vegetables that didn't last more than a day. The details were arcane to me, but it was a government programme, which, somehow, was making them both very rich.

'I work with an Arab,' I said. 'We have a store.'

The registrar nodded severely, as if processing this critical information. 'The Arabs are very able businessmen,' he said finally. 'You must learn everything you can from this Arab.'

'I intend to.'

'So you can be rich!'

'That's the idea,' I said.

A smile flashed across Juan's face. 'And the American girls? Ehhhhh?'

His voice rose with this last drawn-out syllable, so that it sounded like the thrum of a small revving motor.

I told him what he wanted to hear, in exactly the sly tone required. 'They're very *affectionate*.'

Juan clapped again. 'Wonderful! Wonderful! These young people,' he said to my father. 'The whole world is right there for them, just ripe for the taking. Tell me, are you happy, young man?'

I had to remind myself he was addressing that version of me that lived in California, that worked with Hassan, the one who was going to be unspeakably wealthy as a result. Not the me who'd never left the country, who wanted to be an actor, but was actually a part-time employee in a copy shop run by a depressive.

'Yes,' I said. 'Yes, I'm very happy.'

Juan smiled broadly, and I knew my part in the conversation was over. He and my father got down to business. The paperwork was prepared, a long stack of forms and obtusely worded declarations, all signed in triplicate, and in a matter of minutes, my great-uncle's house was officially no longer our problem. I stood when my father did. Juan took my hand, and shook it vigorously.

'California!' he said again, as if he didn't quite believe it.

Once we were free of Juan and the municipal offices, outside again and breathing the briny, life-giving sea air, I congratulated my old man. I said: 'Now we don't have to burn the house down.'

He gave me a weary look. 'Now we can't, you mean.'

We walked towards the plaza. It was late afternoon, still hours of light remaining, but where else could one go in this town? The regulars would be in their habitual spots, waiting for the sunset with steadfast, unflagging patience. It had been barely a day, but already I could understand why my father had fled this place the moment he had the chance. He'd gone first to the provincial capital, a nice enough place which he began to outgrow the moment he arrived. He was young; he wanted more. He moved to the capital itself, where he finished his education, won more prizes, married and went abroad, fulfilling, if only partially, the expectations of those he'd left behind. They'd wanted him to be a judge, or a diplomat, or an engineer. To build bridges or make law. His actual job – head librarian of the antiquarian books and rare manuscripts section of the National Library – was a wholly inconceivable occupation. It sounded less like work one did for a wage, and more like an inherited title of nobility. But then it was precisely the rarefied nature of his position that gave my father such prestige in these parts.

We hadn't gone far when he said, 'Quite the act in there.'

I was feeling good, and opted not to listen for any trace of sarcasm. Instead I thanked him.

'An Arab?' he said. 'A store? How precise!'

'Everything's an act, right? I was improvising. You have to say the lines like you mean them.'

'I see your studies at the Conservatory have really paid dividends. It was very convincing.'

'Your best friend thought so.'

'Best friend, indeed,' my old man said. 'I suppose it's obvious, but I have no memory of him.'

I nodded. 'I don't think he noticed, if that's what you're worried about.'

We still hadn't returned to the discussion of the previous night, and now there seemed no point. Instead we'd come to the plaza, with its view of the sea and its benches filling up one by one. We ducked into a tiny restaurant, hoping to have a quiet meal alone, but everyone recognized my father, and so the basic ritual of our stay in town began anew. We entered the dining room, waving, accepting greetings. A few men called my father's name excitedly – Manuel! Manolito! – and by the way his face shifted, the way his eyes darkened, I could see this prominence beginning to weigh on him. I saw him draw a deep breath, as if preparing for a steep climb. He was bored with it all, though every instinct told him he must bury this cynicism, ignore it. There are no cynics in this town – that is something you learn when you travel. When you live in the capital and become corrupt. One cannot be rude to these people, one cannot make fun of them. They know almost nothing about you any more, but they love you. And this was the bind my old man was in. The night demanded something, some way to shift its course; and perhaps this was why, when we approached the table that had called us, he threw an arm over my shoulder, squeezed me tightly, and introduced me as his son, Nelson, home from abroad.

'From California,' my father said. 'Just back for a visit.'

His announcement caught me by surprise. I hadn't intended to reprise the role debuted in Juan's office, but now there was no choice. I scarcely had a moment to glance in my old man's direction, to catch sight of his playful smile, before a couple of strangers wrapped me in a welcoming embrace. Everything happened quite quickly. A few narrow wooden tables were pushed together; my father and I pressed into perversely straight-backed chairs. We were surrounded. Everyone wanted to say hello; everyone wanted to get a look at me. I shook a dozen hands, grinning the entire time like a politician. I felt very grateful to my old man for this opportunity. It was – how do I explain this? – the role I'd been preparing for my entire life.

Scene: A dim restaurant off the plaza, in a small town on the southern coast. Santos (fifteen or twenty years older than the others, whom they call Profe) and his protégé, Cochocho, do most of the talking; Erick and Jaime function as a chorus, and spend most of their energy drinking. They've been at it all afternoon when an old friend, Manuel, arrives with his son, Nelson. It is perhaps two hours before dark. Manuel lives in the capital, and his son is visiting from the United States. The young man is charming, but arrogant, just as they expect all Americans to be. As the night progresses, he begins to grate on them, something evident at first only in small gestures. Bottles of beer are brought to the table, the empties are taken away, a process as fluid and automatic as the waves along the beach. How they are drained so quickly is not entirely clear. It defies any law of physics. The waitress, Elena, is an old friend too, a heavyset woman in her late forties, dressed in sweatpants and a loose-fitting T-shirt; she observes these men with a kind of pity. Over the years, she has slept with all of them. A closely guarded secret; they are men of ordinary vanity, and each of the four locals thinks he is the only one. Elena's brown-haired daughter, Celia, is a little younger than the American boy – he's in his early twenties – and she lingers in the background, trying to catch a glimpse of the foreigner. Her curiosity is palpable. There are dusty soccer trophies above the bar, and a muted television, which no one watches. Occasionally the on-screen image lines up with the dialogue, but the actors are not aware of this.

NELSON: That's right. California. The Golden State.
ERICK: Hollywood. Sunset Boulevard.
COCHOCHO: Many Mexicans, no?

ERICK: Route 66. James Dean.

JAIME: I have a nephew in Las Vegas. Is that California?

COCHOCHO (*after opening a bottle of beer with his teeth*): Don't answer him. He's lying. He doesn't even know where Las Vegas is. He doesn't know where California is. Ignore him. Ignore the both of them. That's what we do.

ERICK: Magic Johnson. The Olympics.

COCHOCHO (*to Erick*): Are you just saying words at random? Do you ever listen to yourself? (*to Nelson*) Forgive him. Forgive us. It's Friday.

NELSON: I understand.

JAIME: Friday is an important day.

ERICK: The day before Saturday.

NELSON: Of course.

JAIME: And after Thursday.

COCHOCHO: As I said, forgive us.

As well as being the oldest of the group, Santos is also the most formal in speech and demeanour. Suit and tie. He's been waiting for the right moment to speak. He imagines everyone else has been waiting for this, too, for their opportunity to hear him.

SANTOS: I'm appalled by all this. This . . . What is the phrase? This lack of discipline. We must be kind to our guest. Make a good impression. Is it very loud in here? Perhaps you don't notice it. I'm sure things are different where you live. Orderly. I was your father's history teacher. That is a fact.

Nelson looks to his father for confirmation. A nod from Manuel.

MANUEL: He was. And I remember everything you taught me, Profe.

SANTOS: I doubt that. But it was my class, I believe, that inculcated in your father the desire to go north, to the capital. I take responsibility for this. Each year, my best students leave. I'm retired now and I don't miss it, but I was sad watching them go. Of course they have their reasons. If these others had been paying any attention at all to history as I taught it, they might have understood the logic of migration. It's woven into the story of this nation. I don't consider this something to celebrate, but they might have understood it as a legacy they'd inherited. They might have been a bit more ambitious.

COCHOCHO: Profe, you're being unfair.

SANTOS (*to Nelson, ignoring Cochocho*): Your father was the best student I ever had.

MANUEL (*sheepishly*): Not true, Profe, not true.

SANTOS: Of course it's true. Are you calling me a liar? Not like these clowns. I taught them all. (*nodding towards Erick, who is pouring himself a glass of beer*) This one could barely read. Couldn't sit still. Even now, look at him. Doesn't even know who the president is. (*Television: generic politician, his corruption self-evident, as clear as the red sash across his chest.*) The only news he cares about is the exchange rate.

ERICK: The only news that matters. I have expenses. A son and two daughters.

COCHOCHO (*to Nelson*): And you can marry either of them. Take one of the girls off his hands, please.

SANTOS: Or the boy. That's allowed over there, isn't it?

NELSON: How old are the girls?

COCHOCHO: Old enough.

NELSON: Pretty?

ERICK: Very.

COCHOCHO (*eyebrows raised, sceptical*): A man doesn't look for beauty in a wife. Rather, he doesn't look *only* for beauty. We can discuss the details later. Right, Erick?

Erick nods absent-mindedly. It's as if he's already lost the thread of the conversation.

SANTOS: So, young man. What do you do there in California?

NELSON (*glancing first at his father*): I have my own business. I work with an Arab. Together we have a store. It's a bit complicated, actually.

SANTOS: Complicated. How's that? What could be simpler than buying and selling? What sort of merchandise is it? Weapons? Metals? Orphans?

Television: in quick succession, a handgun, a barrel with a biohazard symbol, a sad-looking child. The child remains on-screen, even after Nelson begins speaking.

NELSON: We began with baby supplies. Milk. Formula. Diapers. That sort of thing. It was a government programme. For poor people.

JAIME: Poor Americans?

NELSON: That's right.

COCHOCHO: Don't be so ignorant. There are poor people there, too. You think your idiot cousin in Las Vegas is rich?

JAIME: He's my nephew. He wants to be a boxer.

COCHOCHO (*to Nelson*): Go on.

NELSON: This was good for a while, but there is – you may have heard. There have been some problems in California. Budgets, the like.

SANTOS (*drily*): I can assure you these gentlemen have not heard.

NELSON: So we branched out. We rented the space next door, and then the space next door to that. We sell clothes in both. We do well. They come every first and fifteenth and spend their money all at once.

JAIME: You said they were poor.

NELSON: American poor is . . . *different*.

SANTOS: Naturally.

COCHOCHO: Naturally.

NELSON: We drive down to Los Angeles every three weeks to buy the inventory. Garment district. Koreans. Jews. Filipinos. Businessmen.

SANTOS: Very well. An entrepreneur.

MANUEL: He didn't learn this from me.

SANTOS: You speak Arabic now? Korean? Hebrew? Filipino?

NELSON: No. My partner speaks Spanish.

COCHOCHO: And your English?

MANUEL: My son's English is perfect. Shakespearean.

COCHOCHO: Two stores. And they both sell clothes.

NELSON: We have Mexicans, and we have blacks. Unfortunately these groups don't get along very well. The Mexicans ignore the blacks who ignore the Mexicans. The white people ignore everyone, but they don't shop with us and so we don't worry about them. We have a store for each group.

SANTOS: But they – they all live in the same district?

Television: panning shot of an East Oakland street scene: International

Boulevard. Mixed crowds in front of taco trucks, tricked-out cars rolling by
very slowly, chrome rims spinning, glinting in the fierce sunlight. Latinas
pushing strollers, black boys in long white T-shirts and baggy jeans, which
they hold up with one hand gripping the crotch.
NELSON: They do. And we don't choose sides.
COCHOCHO: Of course not. You're there to make money. Why would
you choose sides?
JAIME: But you live there too? With the blacks? With the Mexicans?
They look him over, a little disappointed. They'd thought he was more
successful. Behind the scene, Elena prepares to bring more beer to the table,
but her daughter stops her, takes the bottles and goes herself.
NELSON: Yes. There are white people, too.
CELIA: Excuse me, pardon me.
Celia has inky black eyes, and wears a version of her mother's outfit – an
old T-shirt, sweatpants, sandals. On her mother, this clothing represents
a renunciation of sexual possibility. On Celia, they represent quite the
opposite.
NELSON: (*eagerly, wanting to prove himself – to the men? to Celia?*) I'd
like to buy a round. If I may.
COCHOCHO: I'm afraid that's not possible. (*Slips Celia a few bills.*) Go
on, dear.
Celia lingers for a moment, watching Nelson, until her mother shoos her
away. She disappears offstage. Meanwhile the conversation continues.
ERICK: You're the guest. Hospitality is important.
SANTOS: These things matter to us. You think it folkloric, or charming.
We're not offended by the way you look at us. We are accustomed to
the *anthropological gaze*. (*This last phrase accompanied by air quotes.*)
We feel sorry for you because you don't understand. We do things a
certain way here. We have traditions. (*to Manuel*) How much does
your boy know about us? About our town? Have you taught him our
customs?
NELSON: I learned the songs when I was a boy.
MANUEL: But he was raised in the city, of course.
COCHOCHO: What a shame. Last time I went was six years ago, when

I ran for Congress. A detestable place. I hope you don't mind my saying that.

MANUEL: Certainly you aren't the only one who holds that opinion.

SANTOS: He wanted very badly to win. He would've happily moved his family there.

JAIME: And your wife, she's from the city?

MANUEL: She is.

COCHOCHO (*to Nelson*): You're lucky to have left. How long have you been in California?

NELSON: Since I was eighteen.

JAIME: It's a terrible place, but still, you must miss home quite a bit.

NELSON (*laughing*): No, I wouldn't say that, exactly.

ERICK: The food?

NELSON: Sure.

JAIME: The family?

NELSON: Yes, of course.

MANUEL: I'm flattered.

JAIME: Your friends?

NELSON (*pausing to think*): Some of them.

ERICK: Times have changed.

SANTOS: No, Erick, times have not changed. The youth are not all that different than before. Take Manuel. Let's ask him. Dear Manuel, pride of this poor, miserable village, tell us: how often do you wake up missing this place where you were born? How often do you think back, and wish you could do it over again, never have left, and stayed here to raise a family?

Manuel is caught off guard, not understanding if the question is serious or not. On the television: a shot of the plaza by night. Quickly recovering, he decides to take the question as a joke.

MANUEL: Every day, Profe.

Everyone laughs but Santos.

SANTOS: I thought as much. Some people like change, they like movement, transition. A man's life is very short and of no consequence. We have a different view of time here. A different way of placing value on things. We find everything you Americans –

NELSON: *We* Americans? But I lived in this country until I was eighteen!

SANTOS (*talking over him*): Everything you Americans say is very funny. Nothing impresses us unless it lasts five hundred years. We can't even begin to discuss the greatness of a thing until it has survived that long. (*It's not clear who Santos is addressing. Still, there's a murmur of approval. His eyes close. He's a teacher again, in the classroom.*) This town is great. The ocean is great. The desert and the mountains beyond. There are some ruins in the foothills, which you surely know nothing about. They are undoubtedly, indisputably, great; as are the men who built them, and their culture. Their blood, which is our blood, and even yours, though unfortunately . . . how shall I put it? *Diluted.* Not great: the highway, the border. The United States. Where do you live? What's that place called?

NELSON: Oakland, California.

SANTOS: How old?

NELSON: A hundred years?

SANTOS: Not great. Do you understand?

NELSON: I'm sure I don't. If I may: those 500-year-old ruins, for example. You'll notice I'm using your word, Profe. *Ruins.* Am I wrong to question whether they've lasted?

Television: the ruins.

SANTOS (*taking his seat again*): You would have failed my class.

NELSON: What a shame. Like these gentlemen?

SANTOS: Nothing to be proud of. Nothing at all.

NELSON (*transparently trying to win them over*): I'd be in good company.

ERICK: Cheers.

JAIME: Cheers.

MANUEL (*reluctantly*): Cheers.

COCHOCHO (*stern, clearing his throat*): I did not fail that class or any class. It's important you know this. I didn't want to mention it, but I am deputy mayor of this town. I once ran for Congress. I could have this bar shut down tomorrow.

ERICK/JAIME (*together, alarmed*): You wouldn't!

COCHOCHO: Of course not! Don't be absurd! (*Pause.*) But I *could*. I am a prominent member of this community.

ERICK: Don't be fooled by his name.

COCHOCHO: It's a nickname! A term of endearment! These two? Their nicknames are vulgar. Unrepeatable. And your father? What was your nickname, Manuel?

MANUEL: I didn't have one.

COCHOCHO: Because no one bothered to give him a name. He was cold. Distant. Arrogant. He looked down on us even then. We knew he'd leave and never come back.

Manuel shrugs. Cochocho, victorious, smiles arrogantly.

NELSON: Here he is! He's returned!

SANTOS: How lucky we are. Blessed.

COCHOCHO: Your great-uncle's old filling station? It's mine now. Almost. I have a minority stake in it. My boy works there. It'll be his some day.

As if reminded of his relative wealth, Cochocho orders another round. No words, only gestures. Again Celia arrives at the table, bottles in hand, as Elena looks on, resigned. This time all the men, including Nelson's father, ogle the girl. She might be pretty after all. She hovers over the table, leaning in so that Nelson can admire her. He does, without shame. Television: a wood-panelled motel room, a naked couple on the bed. The window is open. They're fucking.

SANTOS (*to Manuel*): Don't take this the wrong way. The primary issue . . . What Cochocho is trying to say, I think, is that some of us . . . We feel abandoned. Disrespected. You left us. Now your son is talking down to us.

NELSON (*amused*): Am I?

MANUEL: Is he?

SANTOS: We don't deserve this, Manuel. You don't remember! (*to the group*) He doesn't remember! (*to Nelson*) Your father was our best student in a generation. The brightest, the most promising. His father – your grandfather, God rest his soul – had very little money, but he was well liked, whereas your great-uncle . . . We tolerated Raúl. For a while he was rich and powerful, but he never gave away a cent. He saw your father had potential, but he wanted him to help run the filling station, to organize his properties, to invest. These were his ambitions. Meanwhile, your father, I believe, wanted to be –

NELSON: A professor of literature. At an American university. We've discussed this.

COCHOCHO: Why not a local one?

Manuel has no response, is slightly ashamed.

SANTOS: Pardon me. It's a very conventional ambition for a bookish young man. Decent. Middle of the road. You had politics?

MANUEL: I did. (*Pause.*) I still do.

SANTOS: A rabble-rouser. An agitator. He made some people here very angry, and the teachers – and I was leader of this concerned group, if I remember correctly – we collected money among us, to send him away. We didn't want to see his talent wasted. Nothing destroys our promising youth more than politics. Did he tell you he won a scholarship? Of course. That's a simpler story. He made his powerful uncle angry, and Raúl refused to pay for his studies. Your grandfather didn't have the money either. We sent him away for his own good. We thought he'd come back and govern us well. We hoped he might learn something useful. Become an engineer. An architect. A captain of industry. (*sadly*) We expected more. We needed more. There's no work here. Jaime, for example. What do you do?

JAIME: Sir?

SANTOS (*impatiently*): I said, what do you do?

JAIME: I'm unemployed. I was a bricklayer.

SANTOS: Erick?

ERICK: I'm a tailor. (*to Nelson, brightly, with an optimism that does not match the mood of the table*) At your service, young man!

SANTOS: See? He made me this suit. Local cotton. Adequate work. I'm on a fixed income. Cochocho. He is deputy mayor. You know that now. But did you know this? The money he just spent on our drinks? That is our money. He stole it like he stole the election. He brings his suits from the capital. We don't say anything about it because that would be rude. And he is, in spite of his questionable ethics, our friend.

COCHOCHO (*appalled*): Profe!

SANTOS: What? What did I say? You're not our friend? Is that what you're alleging?

Cochocho, dejected, unable or unwilling to defend himself. Erick and Jaime comfort him. Just then, Elena's daughter reappears, eyes on Nelson. Television: motel room, naked couple in an acrobatic sexual position, a yogic balancing act for two, a scramble of flesh, such that one can't discern whose legs belong to whom, whose arms, how his and her sexual organs are connecting or even if they are.

CELIA: Another round, gentlemen?

MANUEL: I insist –

NELSON: If you'll allow me –

SANTOS (*stopping them both with a wave, glaring at Cochocho*): So, are you our friend or not? Will you spend our money or keep it for yourself? (*to Nelson*) Unfortunately, this, too, is tradition.

NELSON: Five hundred years?

SANTOS: Much longer than that, boy.

NELSON: Please. I'd consider it an honour to buy a round.

Cochocho (*still angry*): Great idea! Let the foreigner spend his dollars!

At this, Nelson stands and steps towards the startled Celia. He kisses her on the mouth, brazenly, and as they kiss, he takes money from his own pocket, counts it without looking, and places it in her hand. She closes her fist around the money, and it vanishes. It's unclear whether he's paying for the drinks or for the kiss itself, but in either case, Celia doesn't question it. The four local men look on, astounded.

SANTOS: Imperialism!

COCHOCHO: Opportunism!

JAIME: Money!

ERICK: Sex!

Manuel stares at his son, but says nothing. Takes a drink. Curtain.

I should be clear about something: it is never the words, but how they are spoken that matters. The intent, the tone. The farcical script quoted above is only an approximation of what actually occurred that evening, after my father challenged me to play Francisco, or a version of him, for this unsuspecting audience. Many other things were said, which I've omitted: oblique insults; charmingly ignorant questions; the occasional reference to one or another invented episode of American history. I improvised, using my brother's letters as a guide, even quoting from them when the situation allowed – the line, for example, about Mexicans ignoring blacks and vice versa. That statement was contained within one of Francisco's early dispatches from Oakland, when he was still eagerly trying to understand the place for himself, and not quite able to decipher the many things he saw.

My most significant dramatic choice was not to defend myself all too vigorously. Not to defend Oakland, or the United States. That would have been a violation of character, whereas this role was defined by a basic indifference to what was taking place. They could criticize, impugn, belittle – it was all the same to me, I thought (my character thought). They could say what they wanted to say, and I would applaud them for it; after all, at the end of the day, I (my character) would be heading back to the US, and they'd be staying here. I needed to let them know this, without saying it explicitly. That's how Francisco would have done it – never entirely sinking into the moment, always hovering above it. Distant. Untouchable.

Through it all, my old man sat very quietly, deflecting attention even when they began discussing him directly, his choices, the meaning and impact of his long exile. I've hurried through the part where my father's friends expressed, with varying levels of obsequiousness, their admiration, their wonder, their jealousy. I've left it out because it wasn't the truth; it was habit – how you treat the prodigal son when he returns, how you flatter him in order to claim some of his success as your own. But this fades. It is less honest, and less interesting than the rest of what took place that night. The surface: Jaime and Erick drank heavily, oblivious and imperturbable

165

to the end, and were for that very reason the most powerful men in the room. I could not say they were any drunker when we left than they were when we arrived. Cochocho, on the other hand, drank and changed dramatically: he became more desperate, less self-possessed, revealing in spite of himself the essential joylessness at the core of his being. His neatly combed hair somehow became wildly messy, his face swollen and adolescent, so that you could intuit, but not see, a grown man's features hidden beneath. No one liked him; more to the point, he did not like himself. And then there was Santos, who was of that generation that catches cold if they leave the house without a well-knotted necktie; who, like all retired, small-town teachers, had the gloomy nostalgia of a deposed tyrant. I caught him looking at Celia a few times with hunger – the hunger of an old man remembering better days – and it moved me. We locked eyes, Santos and I, just after one of these glances; he bowed his head, embarrassed, and looked down at his shoes. He began to hate me, I could feel it. He expressed most clearly what the others were unwilling to acknowledge: that the visitors had upset their pride.

We'd reminded them of their provincialism.

Which is why I liked Santos the best. Even though the role I was inhabiting placed us at opposite ends of this divide; in truth, I identified very closely with this wounded vanity. I felt it, would feel it, would come to own this troubling sense of dislocation myself. I knew it intimately: it was how the real Nelson felt in the presence of the real Francisco.

Hurt. Small.

Now the lights in the bar hummed, and the empty beer bottles were magically replaced with new ones, and my father's old history teacher aged before my eyes, the colour draining from him until he looked like the people in Raúl's old photographs. Jaime and Erick maintained the equanimity of statues. Cochocho, with his ill humour and red, distended skin, looked like the mould spreading on Raúl's kitchen wall. He'd removed his suit jacket, revealing dark rings of sweat at the armpits of his dress shirt. He asked about my great-uncle's house, and when my father said he'd transferred the property to a cousin of ours, the deputy mayor responded with a look of genuine disappointment.

'You could have left it to your son,' he said.

It wasn't what he really meant, of course: Cochocho probably had designs on it himself, some unscrupulous plan that would net him a tidy profit. But I played along, as if this possibility had just occurred to me.

'That's true,' I said, facing my old man. 'Why didn't you?'

My father chose this moment to be honest. 'I didn't want to burden you with it.'

And then the night began to turn. my old man frowned as soon as the words had escaped. It was more of a grimace, really, as if he were in pain; and I thought of those faces professional athletes make after an error, when they know the cameras are on them: they mime some injury, some phantom hurt to explain their mistake. It's a shorthand way of acknowledging, and simultaneously deflecting, responsibility. We sat through a few unpleasant moments of this, until my father forced a laugh, which sounded very lonely because no one joined him in it.

'A burden, you say?'

This was Santos, who, excluding a year and a half studying in France, had lived in the town for all of his seventy-seven years.

Just then Celia came to the table with two fresh bottles. 'Sit with us,' I said. I blurted this out on impulse, for my sake and my father's, just to change the subject. She smiled coquettishly, tilting her head to one side, as if she hadn't heard correctly. Her old T-shirt was stretched and loose, offering the simple line of her thin neck, and the delicate ridge of her collarbone, for our consideration.

'I would love to,' Celia said, 'but it appears there is no room here for a lady.'

She was right: we were six drunken men pressed together in a crowded, unpleasant rectangle. If more than two of us leaned forward, our elbows touched. It was a perfect answer, filling us all with longing, and though we hurried to make room, Celia had already turned on her heels and was headed back to the bar. She expected us to stay for many hours longer, was confident she'd have other opportunities to tease us. Her mother glared at her.

But the men hadn't forgotten my father's insult.

'Explain,' said Santos.

My old man shook his head. He wore an expression I recognized: the same distant gaze I'd seen that first night, when we'd sat up, drinking tea, and looking through Raúl's old photographs. Who are these people? What do they have to do with me? He wasn't refusing; he simply found the task impossible.

I decided to step in, playing the one card my father and I both had.

'I think I know what my old man is trying to get at,' I said. 'I believe I do. And I understand it because I feel the same way towards the capital. He meant no offence, but you have to understand what happens, over time, when one leaves.'

Santos, Cochocho and the others gave me sceptical looks. Nor, it should be said, did my father seem all that convinced. I went on anyway.

'Let's take the city, for example. I love that place – I realize that's a controversial statement in this crowd, but I do. Listen. I love its grey skies, its rude people, its disorder, its noise. I love the stories I've lived there, the landmarks, the ocean, which is the same as the ocean here, by the way. But now, in spite of that love, when I have a son, I would not *leave* it to him. I would not say: here, boy, take this. It's your inheritance. It's yours. I would not want him to feel obligated to love it the way I do. Nor would that be possible. Do you understand? Does that make sense? He'll be an American. I have no choice in the matter. That's a question of geography. And like Americans, he should wake into adulthood and feel free.'

I sat back, proud of my little speech.

'Ah!' Santos said. It was a guttural sound, a physical complaint, as if I'd injured him. He scowled. 'Rank nationalism,' he said. 'Coarse jingoism of the lowest order. Are you saying we're not free?'

We fell silent.

For a while longer the bottles continued to empty, almost of their own accord, and I felt I was perceiving everything through watery, unfocused eyes. The television had been trying to tell me something all night, but its message was indecipherable. I was fully Francisco now. That's not true – I was an amalgam of the two of us, but I felt as close to my brother then as I had in many years. Most of it was internal, and could not have been expressed with any script, with any set of lines. But this audience – I thought back to the two antagonists and Joselito's moto-taxi, the way they became fully invested in the scene the moment they realized they were being watched. I'd taken my brother's story and amplified it. Made it mine, and now theirs, for better or for worse. It was no longer a private argument, but a drama everyone had a stake in. I felt good. Content. Seized by that powerful sense of calm one has when you have understood a character, or rather, when you feel that a character has understood you. I felt very confident, very brash, like I'd imagined my brother had felt all these many years on his journey across North America.

I stood then, and confirmed what I'd begun to sense while seated: I was very drunk. It was comforting in a way, to discover that all that drinking had not been done in vain. It was time to go. Celia and her mother came out from behind the bar, to clear off the table, and the other men stood as well. And this was the moment I as Francisco, or perhaps Francisco as me, pulled Celia close, and kissed her on the mouth. Perhaps this was what the television had been trying to tell me. She kissed me back. I heard the men call out in surprise, heard Celia's mother as well, shrill and protective, but entirely reasonable. After all, who was this young man? And just what did he think he was doing?

I placed one hand at the small of Celia's back, pulling her into me. The crowd continued to voice its disapproval, scandalized, but also – I felt certain – glad for us. The dance is complete. The virile foreigner has made his mark. The pretty girl has claimed her property. And it was the role of the gathered men to be appalled, or to pretend to be; the role of the mother to wail about her daughter's chastity when she herself had never been chaste. But when it was over, when Celia and I separated, everyone was grinning. The old men, my father, even Elena.

Very late that night I called Rocío. I did not feel any guilt. I just wanted to talk to her, perhaps have her read me the letter I'd already imagined. Be amused by her. Perhaps laugh and discuss her lover's murder. It must have been three or four in the morning, and I could not sleep. I'd begun to have doubts about what had happened, what it meant. A few hours before, it had all seemed triumphant; now it felt abusive. The plaza was empty, of course, just like the previous night; only more so – a kind of emptiness that feels eternal, permanent. I knew I would never come back to this place, and that realization made me a little sad. From where I stood, I could see the sloping streets, the ocean, the unblinking night; and nearer, the listing palm tree scarred with names. I would have written Celia's name on it – a useless, purely romantic gesture, to be sure – but the truth is I never knew her name. I've chosen to call her Celia because it feels disrespectful to address her as *the barwoman's daughter*. So impersonal, so anonymous. A barwoman's daughter tastes of bubblegum and cigarettes; whereas Celia's warm tongue had the flavour of roses.

Santos and Cochocho and Jaime and Erick left us soon after the kiss, and it was just me and my father, still feeling amused by what had happened, what we'd been a part of. We maybe felt a little shame, too, but we didn't talk about it because we didn't know how. Grown men with hurt feelings are transparent creatures; grown men who feel dimly they have done something wrong are positively opaque. It would've been much simpler if we'd all just come to blows. Santos and Cochocho wandered off, a bit dazed, as if they'd been swindled. My father and I did a quick circle around the plaza, and begged off for the evening. We never ate. Our hunger had vanished. I tried and failed to sleep, spent hours listening to my father's snores echoing through the house. Now I punched in the numbers from the phonecard, and let it ring for a very long time. I wasn't drunk any more. I liked the sound because it had no point of origin; I could imagine it ringing in the city, in that apartment I shared with Rocío (where she was asleep and could not hear, or was perhaps out with friends on this weekend night), but this was pure fantasy. I was not hearing that ring at all, of course. The ringing I heard came from inside the line, from somewhere within the wires, within the phone, an echo of something mysterious emerging from an unfixed and floating territory.

I waited for a while, listening, comforted; but in the end, there was no answer.

We left the next morning; locked the house, dropped the key in the neighbour's mail slot, and fled quickly, almost furtively, hoping to escape without having to say goodbye to anyone. I had a pounding headache, and I'd barely slept at all. We made it to the filling station at the top of the hill without attracting notice, and then paused. My father was at the wheel, and I could see this debate flaring up within him – whether to stop and fill the tank, or head north, away from this place and what it represented. Even the engine had doubt; it would not settle on an idling speed. We stopped. We had to. There might not be another station for many hours.

It was Cochocho's son tending the pumps. He was a miniature version of his father: the same frown; the same fussy irritation with the world. Everyone believes they deserve better, I suppose; and in this respect, he was no different from me. Still, I disliked him intensely. He had fat, adolescent hands, and wore clothes that could have been handed down from Celia's mother.

'So you're off then?' the boy said to my father through the open window.

The words were spoken without a hint of friendliness. His shoulders tensed, his jaw set in an expression of cold distrust. There was so much disdain seeping towards us, so determined and intentional, I almost found it funny. I felt like laughing, though I knew this would only make matters worse. Part of me – a large part – didn't care: my chest was full of that big-city arrogance, false, pretentious and utterly satisfying. The boy narrowed his eyes at us, but I was thinking to myself:

Goodbye, sucker!

'Long drive,' said Cochocho's son.

And I heard my father say, 'A full day, more or less.'

Then Cochocho's son, to me: 'Back to California?'

I paused. Remembered. Felt annoyed. Nodded. A moment prior I'd decided to forget the boy, had dismissed him, disappeared him. I'd cast my eyes instead down the hill, at the town and its homes obscured by a layer of fog.

'That's right,' I said, though California felt quite far away – as a theory, as a concept, to say nothing of an actual place where real human beings might live.

'I used to work here, you know,' my old man offered.

The boy nodded with sublime disinterest. 'I've heard that,' he said.

The tank was filled, and an hour later we were emptying our pockets for the bored, greedy soldiers. They were the age of Cochocho's son, and just as friendly. Three hours after that, we were passing through Joselito's hometown, in time to see a funeral procession; his, we supposed. It moved slowly alongside the highway, a sombre cloud of grey and black, anchored by the doleful sounds of an out-of-tune brass band. The two men who'd fought over the moto-taxi now stood side by side, holding one end of the casket and quite obviously heartbroken. Whether or not they were acting now, I wouldn't dare to speculate. But I did ease the car almost to a stop; and I did roll my window down and ask my old man to roll down his. And we listened to the band's song, with its impossibly slow melody, like time stretched thin. We stayed there a minute, as they marched away from us, towards the cemetery. It felt like a day. Then we were at the edge of the city; and then we were home, as if nothing had happened at all. ■

GRANTA

THE BEGINNER'S GOODBYE

Anne Tyler

There used to be a dairy outlet over on Reisterstown Road, with a lighted white glass sign outside reading FIRST WITH THE CARRIAGE TRADE. It showed the silhouette of a woman wheeling a baby carriage — a witticism, I guess — and she was just *galloping* along, taking huge confident strides in a dress that flared below her knees although we were in the era of miniskirts. Whenever my family drove past that sign, I thought of my sister. This was before my sister had reached her teens, even, but still I thought of her, for Nandina seemed to have been born lanky, and ungainly, and lacking in all fashion sense. I'm not saying she was unattractive. She had clear grey eyes, and excellent skin and shiny brown hair that she wore pulled straight back from her forehead with a single silver barrette. But the barrette tells you everything: she wore it still, although she would be forty on her next birthday. An ageing girl, was what she was, and had been from earliest childhood. Her shoes were Mary Janes, as flat as scows in order to minimize her height. Her elbows jutted like coat hangers, and her legs descended as straight as reeds to her ping pong-ball ankle bones.

She drove me home from the hospital the afternoon that Dorothy died, and I sat beside her envying her imperviousness. She kept both hands on the steering wheel at the ten and two o'clock positions, just as our father had taught her all those years ago. Her posture was impeccable. (She had never been one of those women who imagine that slouching makes them look shorter.) At first she attempted some small talk – hot day, no rain in the forecast, pity the poor farmers – but when she saw that I wasn't up to it, she stopped. That was one good thing about Nandina. She wasn't bothered by silence.

We were travelling through the blasted wasteland surrounding Hopkins, with its boarded-up row houses and trash-littered sidewalks, but what I mainly noticed was how healthy everyone was. That woman yanking her toddler by the wrist, those teenagers shoving each other off the kerb, that man peering stealthily into a parked car: there was nothing physically wrong with them. A boy standing at an intersection had so much excess energy that he bounced from foot to foot as he waited for us to pass. People looked so robust, so indestructible.

I pivoted to peer out the rear window at Hopkins, its antique dome and lofty pedestrian bridges and flanks of tall buildings – an entire, complex city rising in the distance like some kind of Camelot. Then I faced forward again.

Nandina wanted to take me to her house. She thought mine wasn't fit to live in. But I was clinging to the notion of being on my own, finally, free from all those pitying looks and sympathetic murmurs, and I insisted on her driving me home. It should have tipped me off that she gave in so readily. Turns out she was figuring I would change my mind once I got there. As soon as we reached my block she slowed down, the better to let me absorb the effect of the twigs and small branches carpeting the whole street – *my* twigs and small branches. She drew to a stop in front of my house and switched off the ignition. 'Why don't I just wait,' she said, 'till you make sure you're going to feel comfortable here?'

For a minute I didn't answer. I was staring at the house. It was true that it was in even worse shape than I had pictured. The fallen tree lay everywhere, not in a single straight line but flung all across the yard as if it had shattered on impact. The whole northern end of the house slumped toward the ground, nearly flattening as it reached the sun porch. Most of the roof was covered with a sheet of bright blue plastic. Jim Rust had arranged for that. I vaguely remembered his telling me about it. The plastic dipped at the ridge pole in a way that reminded me of the dip in Dorothy's chest when the rescuers carried her out, but never mind; don't think about that; think about something else. I turned to Nandina and said, 'I'll be fine. Thanks for the lift.'

'Maybe I should come in with you.'

'Nandina. Go.'

She sighed and switched the ignition back on. I gave her a peck on the cheek – a concession. (I'm not usually so demonstrative.) Then I heaved myself out of the car and shut the door and strode off.

It took a moment before I heard her drive away, but she did, finally.

Just in case some of the neighbours were watching from their windows, I made a point of approaching the house like any other man heading home after an outing. I stabbed the front sidewalk briskly with my cane; I glanced around at the fallen branches with mild interest. I unlocked my front door, opened it, shut it behind me. Sagged back against it as if I'd been kicked in the stomach.

An eerie blue light filled the hall, from the blue tarp overhead that showed through the gaps in the ceiling. The living room was too much of a jungle to navigate, and of course I didn't even try to look beyond it to the sun porch. I stepped across a floorful of mail and made my way to the rear of the house. In the kitchen I was relieved to find only a scattering of wood chips on every surface, and one broken windowpane where a stray twig had poked through. But the dining room, to the right, was a ruin. I closed the door again after the briefest glance inside. That was OK, though. A person could live just fine without a dining room! I could eat in the kitchen. I went over to the sink and turned the tap on. Water flowed immediately.

In the bottom of the sink sat a mug, the interior glazed with dried honey and stippled with bark dust, a teaspoon slanting out of it.

Sometimes the most recent moments can seem so long, long ago.

I walked back through the hall to check the guest room, the bathroom and our bedroom. All fine. Maybe I could turn the guest room into a makeshift living room while I was having repairs done. In the shower stall I found a grasshopper. I let it stay where it was. In the bedroom I was tempted to lie down and simply crash – not so much sleep as tumble into unconsciousness – but I didn't give in. I had an assignment to complete. I went to Dorothy's side of the bed and pulled open the drawer of her nightstand. My fear was that she had taken her address book to the sun porch, which sometimes happened; but no, there it lay, underneath an issue of *Radiology Management*.

Her family's name was Rosales. (It was her name, too. She hadn't changed it when we married.) There were several Rosaleses in the address book, all written in Dorothy's jagged, awkward hand, but the one I settled on was Tyrone, her eldest brother. He'd become head of the family after her father died, and I figured that if I phoned him I wouldn't have to phone the others. I also figured that, with luck, I might get Tyrone's wife instead, since in Texas it was barely past midday and Tyrone himself would most likely be at work. I had never met Tyrone or his wife, either one – or anybody else in the family, for that matter – but it seemed to me that a mere sister-in-law would be less subject to some sort of emotional reaction. I was very concerned about the possibility of an emotional reaction. Really I didn't want to make this call at all. Couldn't we just go on as if nothing had happened, since Dorothy never saw her family anyhow? Who would be the wiser? But Nandina had told me I had to do it.

The phone at the other end rang three times, which was long enough for me to start hoping for an answering machine. (Although I knew full well that it would be wrong to leave a mere message.) Then a sharp click. 'Hello?' A man's voice, low and growly.

'Tyrone Rosales?'

'Who's this?'

'This is – this is –'

Of all times, of all impermissible times, I was going to have my speech problem. I made myself go quiet. I took a deep breath. 'Aaron,' I said very slowly. I have more success with *A* words, as long as I slide into them without any hard-edged beginning. 'Woolcott' felt as if it might present difficulties, though, so I said, 'Your b-b-broth–'

'Aaron, *Dorothy's* husband?' he asked.

'Mm-hmm.'

'What's up?'

I took another breath.

'Is something wrong with her?' he asked.

I said, 'A t-t-t- a tree fell on the house.'

Silence.

'A tree fell on the house,' I said again.

'Is she OK?'

I said, 'No.'

'Is she dead?'

I said, 'Yes.'

'Oh,' Tyrone said. 'Good God.'

I waited for him to absorb it. Besides, it felt restful, not talking.

Finally he said, 'When's the service?'

'There won't – won't – no service.'

Nandina and I had already decided. And no burial either; just cremation. I thought Dorothy would prefer that.

Tyrone said, 'No service.'

A pause.

'She was raised religious,' he said.

'Yes, but –'

It seemed best to leave it at that: Yes, but.

'Well,' Tyrone said after a minute, 'anyhow, it wouldn't've been so easy for us to leave the animals.'

'Right.'

'Did she suffer?'

'No!'

I took another breath.

'No,' I said. 'She did not suffer.'

'She always was real spunky. Real mind of her own.'

'It's true.'

'I remember once when we were kids, me and the others were chewing soft tar from the road on this really hot day and Dorothy comes along and we say, "Here, Dorothy, try some." She says, "Are you kidding?" Says, "Why would I want to eat a *highway*?"'

That sounded like Dorothy, all right. I could hear her saying it.

Dorothy as a child had always seemed unimaginable, but now I could imagine her clearly.

'She was named for the girl in *The Wizard of Oz*,' Tyrone said. 'I guess she mentioned that.'

'Oh. No, she didn't.'

'That was our grandpa's idea. He was the one who named all of us. He wanted to make sure we sounded American.'

'I see.'

'So,' he said. 'Anyhow. Thanks for the phone call. Sorry for your loss.'

'I'm sorry for *your* loss,' I told him.

After that, there was nothing more for us to say. Although I felt this odd reluctance to let him hang up. For a while there, while he was talking, Dorothy had been her old self again: strong-willed and sturdy and stubborn. Not the passive victim she had become in her final days.

Each evening when I came home from work, I'd find offerings of food waiting on my front stoop. I believe my neighbours had arranged some sort of rotation system among themselves, although they were clearly overestimating my daily intake. There were foil baking tins and styrofoam takeout boxes and CorningWare casserole dishes (which unfortunately would need washing and returning), all lined up in a row and plastered with strips of adhesive tape letting me know whom to thank. *Thinking of you! The Ushers.* And *Bake uncovered at 350° till brown and bubbling, Mimi.* I would unlock the front door and bend to manoeuvre it all inside. From there I conveyed the items one by one to the kitchen, leaving my cane behind whenever I needed both hands for something spillable. I set everything next to the sink before I began adding to the list I kept on the counter. A column of previous offerings nearly filled the page: *Sue Borden – devilled eggs. Jan Miller – some kind of curry.* The earliest names were crossed out to show I'd already sent thank-you notes to them.

After I'd recorded each dish, I dumped it in the garbage. I hated to waste food, but my refrigerator was packed to the gills and I didn't know what else to do. So the chicken salad, the ziti casserole, the tomatoes with pesto – dump, dump, dump. You could think of it as eliminating the middleman: straight from stoop to trash bin, without the intermediate pause on the kitchen table. Occasionally, abstractedly, I would intercept a drumstick or a spare rib and gnaw on it as I went about my work. While I rinsed out a Pyrex baking dish, I made my way through a cheesecake parked beside the sink, although I didn't much like cheesecake and this one was getting slimier every time I reached for a chunk with my wet fingers. And then all at once I was stuffed and my teeth had that furred feel from eating too much sugar, even though I hadn't sat down to an actual meal.

I dried the baking dish and set it out on the stoop with a Post-it attached: *MIMI*. Outside it was barely twilight, that transparent green kind of twilight you see at the end of a summer day, and I could hear children calling and a wisp of music from a passing car radio. I stepped back into the hall and closed the door.

Next, the mail, which shingled the hall floor and posed a hazard to life and limb every time I stepped over it. I gathered it all up and took it back to the kitchen. The kitchen was my living room now. I'd done nothing about my plans to alter the guest room. I used the table as my desk, with my chequebook and my address book and various stationery supplies arranged in a row across one end. Oh, I was keeping up with my responsibilities admirably! I paid my bills the day they arrived, not waiting for the due dates. I promptly filed catalogues and flyers in the recycling bin. I opened every sympathy note and read it with the utmost care, because there was always the chance that somebody would give me an unexpected glimpse of my wife. Somebody from her workplace, for instance: *Dr Rosales was extremely qualified, and she will be missed at the Radiology Centre.* Well, that was an added viewpoint that I very much appreciated. Or a former patient: *I was so sorry to read about ~~the death of your your loss~~ Dr Rosales in the paper. She was very helpful to me after I had my ~~mastecto~~ surgery, answering all my questions and treating me ~~so normally so ordinarily~~ with dignity.* I suspected that this was a first draft mailed by mistake, but that just made it all the more meaningful, because it revealed the patient's sincerest feelings. She had valued the same qualities in Dorothy that I had valued: her matter-of-fact attitude; her avoidance of condescension. That was the Dorothy I'd fallen in love with.

I answered each note immediately.

Dear Dr Adams,
Thank you so much for your letter. You were very kind to write.

Sincerely,
Aaron Woolcott

Dear Mrs Andrews,
Thank you so much for your letter. You were very kind to write.

Sincerely,
Aaron Woolcott

Then on to the food brigade:

Dear Mimi,
Thank you so much for the ziti casserole. It was delicious.

Sincerely,
Aaron

Dear Ushers,
Thank you so much for the cheesecake. It was delicious.

Sincerely,
Aaron

After that, the housework. Plenty to keep me busy there.

Sweeping the front hall, first. That was unending. Every morning when I woke up and every evening when I came home, a fresh layer of white dust and plaster chips covered the hall floor. Occasionally there were also tufts of matted grey fuzz. What on earth? An outmoded type of insulation, I decided. I stopped sweeping and peered up into the rafters. It was a sight I looked quickly away from, like someone's innards.

And then the laundry, exactly twice a week – once for whites and once for colours. The first white load made me feel sort of lonely. It included two of Dorothy's shirts and her sensible cotton underpants and her seersucker pyjamas. I had to wash and dry and fold them and place them in the proper drawers and align the corners and pat them down and smooth them flat. But the loads after that were easier. This wasn't an unfamiliar task, after all. It used to fall to whichever one of us felt the need of fresh clothing first, and that was most often me. Now I liked going down the stairs to the cool, dim basement, where there wasn't the least little sign of the oak tree. Sometimes I hung around for a while after I'd transferred the wet laundry from the washer to the dryer, resting my palms on the dryer's top and feeling it vibrate and grow warm.

Then a bit of picking up in the kitchen and the bedroom. Nothing major. Dorothy had been the clutterer in our family. By now I had retrieved several pieces of her clothing from around the room, and I'd returned her comb and her hay-fever pills to the medicine cabinet. I made no attempt to discard things. Not yet.

Over the course of an evening the phone would ring several times, but I always checked the caller ID before I picked up. If it was Nandina, I might as well answer. She would arrive at my door in person if I didn't let her know I was still among the living. But the Millers, always after me to go to the symphony with them, or the eternal Mimi King . . . Fortunately, I'd had the good sense to deactivate the answering machine. For a while I'd left it on, and the guilty burden of unreturned calls almost did me in before I remembered the OFF button.

'I'm fine,' I'd tell Nandina. 'How are *you* since five o'clock when I last saw you?'

'I can't imagine how you're coping there,' she would say. 'Where do you sit, even? How do you occupy your evening?'

'I have several places to sit, and no shortage of occupations. In fact, at this very minute I – oh-oh! Gotta go!'

I would hang up and look at my watch. Only eight o'clock?

I angled my wrist to make sure the second hand was still moving. It was.

The earliest bedtime I allowed myself was 9 p.m. I told myself I would read a while before I turned out the light; I wouldn't go to sleep immediately. I had a huge, thick biography of Harry Truman that I'd begun before the accident. But I couldn't seem to make much headway in it. 'Reading is the first to go,' my mother used to say, meaning that it was a luxury the brain dispensed with under duress. She claimed that after my father died, she never again picked up anything more demanding than the morning paper. At the time I had thought that was sort of melodramatic of her, but now I found myself reading the same paragraph six times over, and still I couldn't have told you what it was about. My eyelids would grow heavier and all at once I'd be jerking awake as the book slid off the bed and crashed to the floor.

So I would reach for the remote control and turn on the TV that sat on the bureau. I would watch – or stare in a glazed way at – documentaries and panel discussions and commercials. I would listen to announcers rattling off the side effects of all the medications they were touting. 'Oh, sure,' I would tell them. 'I'll run out and buy that tomorrow. Why let a little uncontrollable diarrhoea put me off, or kidney failure, or cardiac arrest?'

Dorothy used to hate it when I talked back like that. 'Do you mind?' she would ask. 'I can't hear a word they're saying.'

This TV was just a little one, the little extra one that we sometimes watched the late news on when we were getting ready for bed. Our big TV was in the sun porch. It was an old Sony Trinitron. Jim Rust told me in the hospital that that was what had crushed Dorothy's chest; the firemen said it had fallen off its bracket high in the corner. Sony Trinitrons are known for their unusual weight.

A while back, Dorothy and I had discussed buying one of those newfangled flat-screen sets, but we'd decided we couldn't afford it. If we had had a flat-screen TV, would Dorothy still be alive?

Or if her patient hadn't cancelled. Then she wouldn't even have been home yet when the tree fell.

Or if she had stayed in the kitchen instead of heading for the sun porch.

If I'd said, 'Let's see if *I* can find those Triscuits,' and gone out to the kitchen to help her look, and then sat with her at the kitchen table while she ate them.

But no, no. I had to stomp off in a huff and sulk in the bedroom, as if it had mattered in the least that she'd refused to settle for Wheat Thins.

Oh, all those annoying habits of hers that I used to chafe at – the trail of crumpled tissues and empty coffee mugs she left in her wake, her disregard for the finer points of domestic order and comfort. Big deal!

Her tendency to make a little too much of her medical degree when she was meeting new people. 'I'm Dr Rosales,' she would say, instead of 'I'm Dorothy', so you could almost see the white coat even when she wasn't wearing one. (Not that she actually met new people all that often. She had never seen the purpose in socializing.)

And those orthopaedic-type shoes she had favoured: they had struck me, at times, as self-righteous. They had seemed a deliberate demonstration of her seriousness, her high-mindedness – a pointed reproach to the rest of us.

I liked to dwell on these shortcomings now. It wasn't only that I was wondering why they had ever annoyed me. I was hoping they would annoy me still, so that I could stop missing her.

But somehow, it didn't work that way.

I wished I could let her know that I'd kept vigil in the hospital. I hated to think she might have felt she was going through that alone.

And wouldn't she have been amused by all these casseroles!

That was one of the worst things about losing your wife, I found: your wife is the very person you want to discuss it all with.

The TV infiltrated my sleep, if you could call this ragged semi-consciousness sleep. I dreamed the war in Iraq was escalating, and Hillary Clinton was campaigning for the Democratic nomination. I rolled over on the remote control and someone all at once shouted, '. . . this stainless-steel, hollow-ground, chef-quality . . .' by which time I was sitting bolt upright in my bed, my eyes popping and my heart pounding and my mouth as dry as gauze. I turned off the TV and lay flat again. I closed my eyes and gritted my teeth: *Go to sleep, dammit.*

You would think I'd have dreamed about Dorothy, but I didn't. The closest I came to it was the whiff of isopropyl alcohol that I hallucinated from time to time as I finally drifted off again. She had carried that scent home on her skin at the end of every workday. Early in our marriage I used to have vivid dreams about childhood doctor visits and vaccinations and the like, evoked by the alcohol scent as I lay sleeping next to her. Now the ghost of it brought me sharply awake, and once or twice I even spoke her name aloud: 'Dorothy?'

But I never got an answer.

The casseroles started thinning out and the letters stopped. Could people move on that easily? Yes, well, of course. New tragedies happened daily. I had to acknowledge that.

It seemed heartless that I should think to go in for my semi-annual dental check-up, but I did. And then I bought myself some new socks. Socks, of all things! So trivial! But all my old ones had holes in the toes.

One evening my friend Nate called – *WEISS N I* on my caller ID. Him, I picked up for. Right off I said, 'Nate! How've you been?' without waiting for him to announce himself. But that was evidently a mistake, because I caught a brief hesitation before he said, 'Hello, Aaron.' Very low-voiced, very lugubrious; not at all his usual style.

'How about a game tomorrow?' I asked him.

'Pardon?'

'A game of racquetball! I'm turning into an old man, here. All my joints are rusting.'

'Well, ah, but . . . I was calling to invite you to dinner,' he said.

'Dinner?'

'Yes, Sonya was saying we ought to have you over.'

Sonya must be his wife. I had never met his wife. I suppose he must have mentioned her now and then, but we didn't have that kind of friendship. We had a *racquetball* friendship. We'd gotten acquainted at the gym.

I said, 'Over to . . . to your house, you mean?'

'Right.'

'Well, gosh, Nate, I don't know. I don't even know where you live!'

'I live in Bolton Hill,' he said.

'And also I just . . . it's been really busy at work lately. You wouldn't believe how busy. I barely have time for a sandwich, and then when I do find time there is so much extra food in the fridge, these – these – these casseroles and these . . . cheesecakes. It's practically a full-time job just to g-g-get it all d-d-d- . . . just to eat it!'

'I see,' he said.

'But thanks.'

'That's OK.'

'Tell Sonya I appreciate the thought.'

'OK.'

I wanted to revisit the racquetball idea, but after I'd made such a point of being busy I figured that would be a mistake. So I just told him goodbye.

Not half an hour later, the phone rang again. This time it was *TULL L*. I answered, but I was warier now. All I said was, 'Hello?'

'Hi, Aaron, it's Luke.'

'Hi, Luke.'

'I can understand why you might prefer not to go to Nate's.'

'Excuse me?'

'He told me you'd turned down his invitation.'

I said, 'You're talking about Nate Weiss.'

'Why, yes.'

'You *know* Nate Weiss?'

'We met in the hospital waiting room, remember? When we both stopped by to visit.'

This had been happening a lot lately. I swear I had no recollection that either one of them had stopped by, let alone that they'd met each other. But I said, 'Oh. Right.'

'He says he got the impression you're not up yet for coming to dinner.'

'No, but racquetball . . .' I said. 'I'm itching for a good game of racquetball.'

There was a pause. Then Luke said, 'Unfortunately, I don't know how to play racquetball.'

'Oh.'

'But I was thinking: if getting together with wives and such is too much to handle just now –'

'*Oh*, no. *Lord*, no,' I said briskly. 'Doesn't faze me in the least.'

Another pause. Then he said, 'I was thinking you could come to the restaurant instead.'

He meant *his* restaurant, the family place he managed for his uncle. I said, 'Well, that's a good idea, Luke. Maybe sometime in the –'

'Just you and me and Nate; just us guys. No wives. We could have an early supper, and then you could head on home whatever time you felt like. How about it?'

I didn't want to do that either, but what could I say? It was nice of him to make the effort. It was nice of both of them. I doubted I would have done as much if I had been in their place. I was more the 'Let's move on' type. The 'Maybe if I don't mention your loss, you'll forget it ever happened' type.

I kind of wished *they* were that type, to be honest.

But OK: might as well get this over with. I met them directly after work the next evening, a rainy, blowy Tuesday in mid-September. It had been pouring all day, and driving conditions were terrible. On top of that, I had trouble finding a parking space. By the time I walked into the restaurant (white linens, wide-planked floors, a certain worn-around-the-edges friendliness), Nate and Luke were already seated at a table. They made an unlikely pair. Nate looked very sleek and dark and professional in his black lawyer suit, while Luke was one of those all-one-colour, beige-hair-beige-skin types in shabby khakis, going a little soft around the middle. They seemed to be having no trouble finding things to talk about, though, if you judged by the way they'd set their heads together. I had the distinct impression that it was me they were talking about. How to deal with me, what topics would be safe to discuss with me. I'd barely pulled my chair out before Nate asked, 'What about this *weather*, hey?' in a sprightly tone I wasn't familiar with. And Luke rode right over the tail of that with, 'You been following the Orioles?'

I felt compelled to answer in kind, in a louder voice than usual and with more verve. 'You know, I *haven't* as a matter of fact been following the Orioles lately,' I said, and then I wanted to take the words back, because I knew they'd be misinterpreted.

Sure enough: Nate said, 'Well, of course you haven't. You've had a lot more important things to think about.'

'No, I just meant –'

'Both of you should try the oysters!' Luke broke in. 'We're in the *R* months now!'

Luke was such a quiet man ordinarily that it was bizarre to see him so animated. Besides which, he clearly felt uneasy sitting idle in his own workplace. He kept glancing around at other tables, raising his eyebrows significantly at waiters, frowning over Nate's head in the direction of the kitchen. 'I personally recommend eating these raw,' he told me in a distracted way, 'but if you prefer, you could order the, uh ' and then he paused to listen to what a short man in a stained apron was whispering in his ear.

' . . . the Oysters Rockefeller,' Nate finished for him. 'Those are great. They use this special slab bacon that comes from upstate New York.'

'You've eaten here before?' I asked.

'Yes, we came by last week,' he said, and then he gave a little grimace, which I couldn't figure out for a moment. Was it because he had let it slip that he and Luke had met earlier, perhaps to cogitate over The Aaron Problem? No, on second thought it must have been the 'we' that had embarrassed him, because next he said, as if correcting himself, 'I had thought after I met him that I'd like to try his food.'

So apparently the plan tonight was to avoid all mention of wives. Pretend neither one of them even possessed a wife. For now Luke, turning back to us as the aproned man left, said, 'Sorry, the chef has run out of lamb chops, is all,' and I happened to know that he was married to the chef. Under ordinary circumstances, he would have said that Jane or Joan or whatever her name was had run out of lamb chops, and he might also have brought her out to introduce her. But these were not ordinary circumstances.

I became perverse. I do that, sometimes. I started mentioning wives right and left – each utterance of the word 'wife' thudding on to our table like a stone. 'Did your wife like the Oysters Rockefeller too?' I asked Nate, and Nate shifted in his seat and said, 'Oh, um . . . she doesn't eat shellfish.'

'You know, I've never thought to wonder,' I said to Luke. 'Did your wife become chef here before you married her, or after?'

'Er, before, actually,' Luke told me. 'Say! We need to decide on the wine!' and he sat forward urgently and beckoned to a waiter.

But I relented, after that, and let the conversation drift into more or less normal channels. Nate turned out to be the food-for-food's-sake type, going on at length about the breeding beds of oysters and the best source for heirloom pork. Luke, whom you'd expect to be deeply concerned with such things, didn't seem all that interested and spent most of his time focusing on what everyone else in the place was eating, or not eating enough of, or looking dissatisfied with. And within a bearable length of time, we managed to get through the evening.

'We should do this again!' Nate said as we were parting, and Luke said, 'Yes! Make a regular thing of it!'

Oh, or else not. But I nodded enthusiastically, and shook both their hands, and thanked Luke for the meal, which he had refused to let us pay for.

I didn't thank either one of them for the event itself – for the act of getting together. That would have implied that it had been a charitable gesture of some sort, and I most certainly was not in need of charity.

So I turned up my collar, and gave both of them a jaunty wave of my cane, and set off through the downpour as cocky as you please.

Though I'd have to say that I felt a little, maybe, woebegone as I drove home alone.

The outside light was supposed to come on automatically at dusk, but the bulb must have burned out. A damned nuisance, in the rain. I stepped in a couple of puddles as I was walking up the sidewalk to my house, and my trouser cuffs were already wet enough as it was. I unlocked the door and reached inside to turn the hall light on, but that was burned out too. And when I pushed the door wider open, I met with some kind of resistance. A gravelly sound startled me. I peered down at the dark hall floor and made out several white and irregular objects. I nudged them with my foot. Rocks? No, plaster, chips of plaster. I pushed the door harder and it opened a few more inches. My eyes had adjusted by now. Against the black of the floor I saw scatterings of white and then a mound of white – pebbles and clods and sheets of white. And now that I thought about it, the air I was breathing was full of dust. I could feel an urge to cough pressing my throat. And I heard a loud, steady dripping from somewhere inside the house.

I closed the door again. I went back to my car, stepping in the same two puddles on the way, and got behind the steering wheel, where I spent several minutes collecting my thoughts. Then I drew a deep, shaky breath and fitted my key into the ignition.

And that is how it happened that I went to live with my sister. ■

At Thirty

At thirty, I fled from my life
in a hailstorm and firestorm, into what
I termed 'the big rest',

unpacked at my mother's house,
slept in my sister's bed,
signed up to swim at the Y, swam twice

daily, in the mornings
with patients doing recovery exercises
in the shallow end,

afternoons hung the damp suit,
black flag, on the line,
microwaved a meal, then napped,

the sleep my calamine, chlorine
my medicine, my weakness everywhere,
I could barely stand,

I swam the evenings, before closing,
reciting poems silently
from the mind's anthology,

I was alone, backstroking
through that humid chamber, beneath
frescoes of dolphins and nymphs,

I floated, a baby in her crib,
mesmerized by those gentle images –
for a long time it was like this.

GRANTA

THE MAGAZINE OF NEW WRITING

SUBSCRIPTION FORM FOR US, CANADA AND LATIN AMERICA

Yes, I would like to take out a subscription to *Granta*.

GUARANTEE: If I am ever dissatisfied with my *Granta* subscription, I will simply notify you, and you will send me a complete refund or credit my credit card, as applicable, for all un-mailed issues.

YOUR DETAILS
MR / MISS / MRS / DR ....
NAME ....
ADDRESS ....
....
CITY... STATE ....
ZIP CODE .... COUNTRY ....
EMAIL ....

☐ Please check this box if you do not wish to receive special offers from *Granta*
☐ Please check this box if you do not wish to receive offers from organizations selected by *Granta*

YOUR PAYMENT DETAILS

1 year subscription: ☐ US: $45.99 ☐ Canada: $57.99 ☐ Latin America: $65.99

3 year subscription: ☐ US: $112.50 ☐ Canada: $148.50 ☐ Latin America: $172.50
Enclosed is my check for $_____ made payable to *Granta*.

Please charge my: ☐ Visa ☐ Mastercard ☐ Amex

Card No. ☐☐☐☐☐☐☐☐☐☐☐☐☐☐☐☐

Exp. ☐☐☐☐

Security Code ☐☐☐☐

SIGNATURE .... DATE ....

Please mail this order form with your payment instructions to:

Granta Publications
PO Box 359
Congers NY 10920-0359

Or call toll free 1-866-438-6150
Or visit GRANTA.COM for details

Source code: BUS118PM

ANECDOTES

Ann Beattie

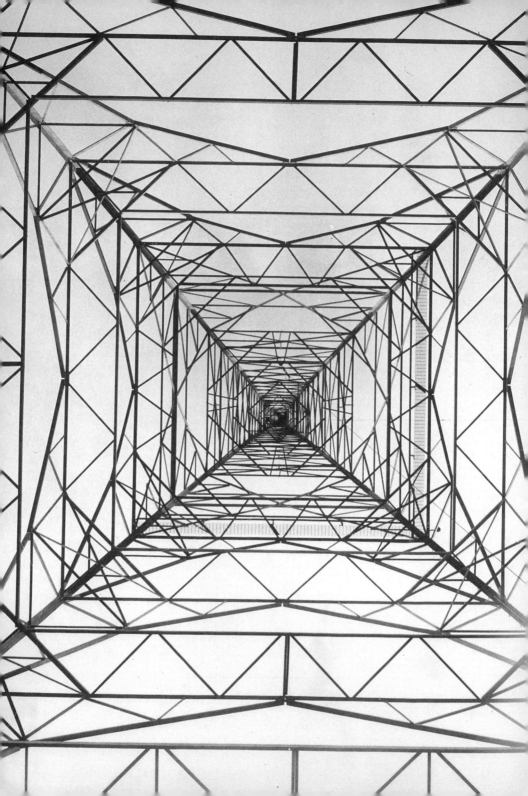

My husband and I were in Tivoli, and we went to the gardens at Villa d'Este. He'd been to Italy before, but it was my first trip. There were rails in front of the fountains because the water was so polluted, they wanted to keep you from being splashed.'

'I went to Italy when they were almost giving shoes away – shoes made of leather as soft as gloves – and there were no tours being given of the Forum. I don't think there was one Japanese tourist in all of Rome. Maybe my trip was before cameras were invented.'

Lucia and I were playing the Italy-One-Upmanship game in the back seat of a Carey car. I knew I was going to be the one to pay the fare. I was doing my friend Christine a favour. Lucia, her mother, had come in from Princeton on the train to hear Christine's talk at Columbia about Margaret Bourke-White. Christine would also be showing slides of newly discovered photographs, printed from Bourke-White negatives that had been mislabelled at *Life*. She was hoping to be hired full-time at Columbia and this was one of several talks she would be giving there and elsewhere, aiming to impress.

Christine had hoped to be a model when she came to the city, but she'd been diagnosed with diabetes shortly thereafter and hadn't been able to keep up the pace. There were still problems with her energy; she felt like she was having what she'd heard were classic menopausal symptoms at thirty-four. She was pretty, though, as you'd imagine. I'd met her in college when we'd been two-timed by the same guy, who also happened to be our professor. I overheard the tantrum she threw, late one evening. I'd gone back to school because I'd forgotten my raincoat, and the forecast was for a weekend of rain. Arthur was in his office; Christine was yelling, and as I came up the stairs, I heard my name mentioned. Loudly. She and I went to a bar when she'd finished confronting him. He went home to his wife. Christine and I lost touch, but met up several years later in New York, when she called to compliment me on an article I'd written for the *New York Times Magazine*.

Earlier in the week Christine had asked me to pick up her mother before she realized that my car was in the repair shop (hit from behind at a red light on West End Avenue), and she probably also called because I did better with her mother, generally, than she did.

'Let me ask you this, Anna,' Lucia said. 'Was there a moment you knew your marriage wasn't going to work, or was it more gradual, the realization?'

'He took the puppy back to the breeder. That didn't help.'

'You always say something unexpected. That's why you're a good writer, I guess. Let me ask this: do you think Christine didn't marry Paul because all her women friends are independent, or do you think she just got tired of him? He sent me a Christmas card, and his heart is still broken.'

I thought, for a moment, about poor broken-hearted Paul. Though ostensibly monogamous for the three-plus years he and Christine lived together, he'd given her herpes. Another thing I knew about him was that he'd put a pillow over his head and stayed in bed the night she had food poisoning. I also thought that when she stopped wearing make-up and pulled her hair back in a French twist, the little tendrils that escaped still didn't make her feminine enough for him. He'd kept a picture of her from her modelling days in his wallet.

'Lucia,' I said, 'I don't think women break up with their boyfriends because other women are without boyfriends.'

'But think: the diabetes made her angry, didn't it? She wanted somebody to take it away. I find significance in the fact that she started to go out with her doctor.'

'You're as funny as I am,' I said. 'Shall I recommend you to my agent?'

'Funny? Nothing funny about that awful disease,' she said, missing my point, because she found it necessary to correct everyone.

'Which side?' the driver said.

'On the right,' I said. 'Far corner.'

He gave me a quick look in the rear-view mirror; the light had just turned red, and by the time he got to the far corner, cars in back of him would start honking the minute he stopped.

The young man setting up the slide projector looked up, thinking one of us must be the speaker. He held a clip-on mike, awkwardly, as if courting someone with a little unwanted flower.

Lucia sat in a chair midway down the aisle. She looked vaguely irritated, or simply tired. She had not wanted Christine to be a model, but neither had she wanted her to be in the academic world, which Lucia felt was full of pseudo-intellectuals hiding from society. As far as I could tell, Lucia had some vague notion that her daughter should be working outside the system, to save the world.

'Wasn't this scheduled for seven?' I said. 'Where is everybody?'

'I'm just here to set up,' the young man said. 'You've got nothing to do with this?'

I shook my head. That was so often my situation with Christine: she insisted I was indispensable, though I had nothing directly to do with what was going on. In school, I hadn't known she was seeing Arthur, but when I found out, she insisted that we have a drink, because only I could fill in the pieces of the puzzle.

Lucia had taken off her enormous scarf – cashmere, certainly – and folded it on her lap, her hands clasped on top. She looked at me with quiet attention, as if I might start singing. Her hair, streaked with silver, was wind-blown. The way the wind had messed up her part made her look less austere. Where Christine had gotten her cheekbones from, and her lips, I couldn't imagine. (Her father had left before Christine began school and I'd only seen him once in a snapshot she carried in her wallet.) Lucia was attractive, but in a quite ordinary way. Like many women her age, she diverted attention from her face by swirling scarves around her throat and shoulders, wearing big necklaces or turtlenecks that seemed like perfect soufflés just lifted from the oven. I was rummaging in my bag, trying to find the piece of paper on which I'd written the time and place. Yes; the talk was taking place here – that's what I'd written down – at 7 p.m.

Suddenly there were voices in the corridor, and students rushed in like horses spooked by firecrackers. There had been another lecture – this was part two of their evening. I stared into the crowd, hoping to see Christine. The person who'd set up the slide projector paced the aisle, talking on his cellphone. The microphone sat in a tangle of wires back on the table.

Lucia beckoned to me. I walked back a few rows, jostled by students – though I noticed none of them had disturbed the elderly lady who sat in the aisle seat, her garments piled in her lap. She had slipped out of her coat, which was a shade somewhere between beige and butter.

'Listen: you have always been such a good friend to Christine that I want to tell you something. Will you sit?' She patted the chair next to her.

Almost none of the students seemed to be wearing winter clothes. A few had on unzipped jackets. I sat next to Lucia, carefully stepping over her elegant shoes.

'Here is what I want to talk about,' Lucia said. 'You remember Thanksgiving in Princeton? I pointed out my neighbour – the lady who had been so sweet on the visiting writer?'

'Vaguely,' I said.

'Vaguely! I made an apple tart from scratch, with crème fraiche!'

'It was delicious. Your meals always are. I just couldn't remember the face of the woman who'd – what? She'd written love notes to him, or something? To the writer?'

'She wanted him to come live there. She said, "Bring your wife, there is a whole separate house. Don't commute the way you do, it will wear you out. I love having young people around. I will teach your wife to cook – whatever she wants." Which is true, by the way. Edwina cooks better than I do.'

'I didn't know all that. I think you whispered to me who she was. That she'd made trouble by writing letters to him, or something.'

'She wrote letters, and he finally came over to have a drink. They hit it off, and he decided he and his wife should take her up on her offer.'

'So what happened?' I said.

'His wife got on a small chartered plane in Michigan, and that was the end of her. It went down in a storm, the pilot killed, everybody. Two other people, I think. And he came over to Edwina's house and picked up bricks from the new walkway that was being laid and threw them through her picture window. The police were called. He was completely crazy. He couldn't ever go back to teach his classes. And Edwina was devastated.'

Christine had come into the auditorium. From nowhere, the man with the tangled microphone charged up to her, getting much too close, so that before she understood who he was, she jumped back. She had a bag bulging with things slung over her shoulder, and carried another bag. It must have started raining, because her hair was matted to her head. A clump of it curved down her cheek like the top of a big question mark. Her earring stud might have been the point that completed the punctuation.

'Your friend shouldn't feel bad,' I said. 'You're right. It wasn't her fault, of course.'

'Yes, but she thinks it was,' Lucia said. She did not follow my eyes to Christine.

I waved. Christine didn't see me at first, but then she did. 'There she is,' I said to Lucia, wondering why she wasn't turning as I waved.

'What I understand of the situation is that he'd slept with Edwina once. She's old enough to be his mother! She was offering her home anyway, so I don't think he was calculating . . .'

A girl and a boy pushed past us, trailing jackets. The girl had on pink Uggs.

I stood to walk toward Christine, who looked a little disoriented. When she saw me, she gave me a nervous smile. She said, 'I washed my hair, and my dryer broke. Can you believe it?'

'That's awful,' I said.

'Thanks for getting her,' Christine said, squeezing my shoulder as she walked past, the microphone already clipped to her lapel, the receptor in her coat pocket. 'Hi, Mom,' she said, smiling, but not bending to kiss her mother's cheek. They were more affectionate privately, I'd noticed. In public, there was some awkwardness.

The row Lucia sat in was almost full. She frowned, as more students pushed past her seat. It was a small auditorium, but this was a good crowd.

Christine stood behind the podium, her coat tossed on a chair, the bags slumped beside it.

'The person who was going to introduce me has laryngitis, so I'm just going to introduce myself – I'm Christine Liss, from the English department – and thank you for coming on such a cold night. There is exciting new work by the eminent photographer Margaret Bourke-White I've gotten access to as it's being catalogued, some of which you'll see tonight. Ms Bourke-White was a fearless photographer who did the first cover for *Life* magazine – a very influential picture magazine of its time, with a reputation that still elicits great respect. She worked downtown, in the then newly built Chrysler Building – a building with a terrace where she kept two small alligators she was given as gifts, until they grew large enough to devour the tortoise she had also been given. Some people wouldn't visit the studio. She was married twice, the last time to Erskine Caldwell, whose name might not be as recognizable to you now as he would have hoped. Her photographs can be seen many places in New York – currently, at ICP Midtown. What you're going to see tonight are mostly aerial shots . . .'

I should probably have returned to sit with Lucia, but I'd trailed Christine halfway down the aisle, and when the lights began to dim, I sat, as if I'd been playing musical chairs. Down the row, someone was videotaping Christine, the little square of light distracting and mesmerizing. Rows back, a cellphone played music and was quickly turned off. The projection screen was filled with aerial views of destruction: Germany, after the war.

Christine's hair had begun to dry, and she looked different, with her hair down and her glasses on. Her earnestness made her look younger, and took me back to the bar where we'd sat in Pennsylvania years ago. Christine cursing Arthur, pulling a necklace with a lapis stone out from under the neckline of her blouse, pulling so hard she broke the chain, the gold puddling on the tabletop, the little stone flashing in the fluorescent light. She had scooped it up and later addressed an envelope to Arthur's wife and mailed it to her without comment.

Slide after slide, when seen from a high vantage point, the world was transformed into abstract art. The photographs were pattern and shape before they became slowly distinguishable as the landscape – the wreckage – they depicted then; as you stared, they devolved into abstraction again, making your eyes skate figure eights. Margaret Bourke-White had no fear of heights, Christine told us, and couldn't have worried about being in a helicopter when she thought nothing of crawling out on the gargoyles atop the Chrysler Building to photograph the city. There she was, bent over her camera, high up, like a steelworker. She photographed machines. She photographed Stalin, who didn't give her an inch until she nervously dropped her flashbulbs, and then he laughed.

Christine talked about industry, mass production. She talked about photographs in black and white, about silver halide crystals, and how photographs were processed. The images at the end of the talk were back in the world – dams and wheels, enormous things. When the lights came on, people applauded. Christine smiled, unclipping the mike, pushing her hair out of her eyes. A few people called out to each other; cellphones appeared immediately, hats and scarves were left behind, picked up by someone else who ran up behind them, like a relay race in reverse. I saw one of Christine's colleagues, whose name I couldn't remember, and said hello. 'God, Bourke-White photographed Stalin's *mother,* you know. I'd think *that* was a dangerous assignment – unless the guy didn't like his mother. And since he didn't like anybody . . .' He shook his head as he passed by to congratulate Christine. The person operating the slide projector was removing the tray, putting it in a box, his cellphone clamped between his chin and shoulder. Lucia stood, her row empty.

'Why do they wear those boots like horse hooves?' she said, looking at the departing students. 'Pastel-pink horse hooves.'

'Comfortable, I guess,' I said. 'Sort of like big bedroom slippers. They love pyjama bottoms, too.'

'It used to be that every generation had its style. I guess this generation's style is what you'd wear if you spent your day in the bedroom. In my day, that would have been a negligee and make-up, which is just as silly, I suppose.'

'What a fascinating talk Christine gave,' I said.

'Too many anecdotes,' Lucia said.

I looked at her, surprised. She was often hard on Christine, but the talk had obviously been so good, I hadn't been expecting such a remark.

'It doesn't matter how many husbands a woman has, or doesn't have. I don't know why she felt she had to mention that,' she said. 'I thought she was going to digress and tell us about the man she loved the most, a soldier she was going to reunite with, except that he was in a military hospital in Italy, and they bombed his wing of the hospital. The other wing was intact, but he was killed instantly.'

'You know about Margaret Bourke-White?' I said.

'I read autobiographies, Anna. It's all there in her book.'

'Well, I thought Christine did a very good job, talking about how Bourke-White got into the workforce, and –'

'Getting the job done is what's important. Not how you got the job.'

'You're too hard on her,' I said.

She looked at me. 'Do you think so? I just don't have much patience with anecdotes.'

'She was explaining that Margaret Bourke-White had a lot of sadness in her life, just like the rest of us.'

'Yes, I think we could assume that everyone experiences sadness,' Lucia replied.

I thought: why do you never offer to pay, like you're a princess? Why not arrange your own transportation in the city? Why don't you cook your own Thanksgiving dinner for fewer people, rather than having two Mexican women in the kitchen all day, and you making only your perfect apple tarts?

My face must have clouded over; she put her hand on my arm and said, 'Sit down for a second. We're friends, you and I. I have something important to tell you.'

I sank, rather than sat. Was she going to tell me she was sick? She had seated herself one chair in, giving me the aisle, gesturing grandly, as if the seat were a gift. The last cluster of students stood talking to Christine.

'You're a writer. Writers have become celebrities, haven't they? Whether they want to be, or not. Well, the visiting writer did want to be the centre of attention, it seemed to me. Writers are so often insecure. So let me tell you: in my one conversation with him, it seems he'd never even heard that Bruce Chatwin hadn't told the whole truth, and nothing but the truth. Didn't know Chatwin had made things up – including the information about what killed him, we now know. If I'd talked about James Frey, I suppose I could have made some of the same points. From what the visiting writer revealed about himself, I thought he was a literary lightweight. I wouldn't have offered him, and his wife, my house. But that's neither here nor there. Edwina, my friend, has been taking one of those mood-altering drugs, and she's calmer now, so she understands she isn't responsible, but you know, she'd gotten to the point where she imagined him and his wife in her house. She imagined them sitting by the fireplace, she looked at her window and saw the shattered glass even though it had been replaced, she saw the dead woman standing in the kitchen doing dishes – she didn't really *see* her, she's not crazy, but she imagined her. I told her, Come to my house. Get out of there; get out of that environment for a while. I guess I did just what she did, didn't I, offering my house? But she was impulsive, and I was her friend of more than twenty-five years. So it came as quite a surprise to both of us that we fell in love. We did. Your eyes are as big as saucers, Anna. If we did, we did.'

I nodded, registering the beginning of a faint headache as I narrowed my eyes.

'Writers like to surprise readers, but they don't like to be surprised, I've found.' She grasped my wrist. 'Here is why I'm telling you: I'm going to tell Christine about it and I think it's going to come as something of a shock for her, so I wanted you to know, before we have our drink. You knew we were going to the Carlyle, where I'm staying tonight, the three of us, to have a drink?'

'I don't think she told me,' I said, though as I spoke, I vaguely remembered Christine saying something. More as a possibility, though. Her phone call to me a couple of days before had been on the run, pleading: 'I've got to teach, then run home and walk Walter, then get back to give the talk, so can you please, *please*, meet her train and see that she gets there OK?'

Lucia could book a room at an expensive hotel, but not offer to pay for the car? She wanted . . . what? For me to be prepared, in case her daughter became (improbably) a basket case, when she told her? I wished she hadn't told me. I wasn't pleased about knowing this information before Christine did. It would make a liar of me if I pretended what I was hearing was news, and I'd be her mother's confidante if I let on that she'd already told me.

'This is private. It's between you and your daughter,' I said. 'I'm going to go home and let you two talk.'

'No, Anna, you have to join us,' she said.

'You want an audience, just like those writers you're so suspicious of,' I said. 'I'd wonder, if I were you, whether he ever slept with your friend, or whether that wasn't her imagination, too. You hear about it when a person has a reputation for sleeping around,' I said. 'I doubt that it's true.'

I had met his wife at a fund-raiser. She'd quickly confessed she felt out of place, and didn't know what to talk about. Her pin had fallen on the floor, that was how we'd met. I'd bent to pick it up, and had helped her fasten it to the collar of her silky black shirt again. When her husband the writer saw us talking, he came up to us. I could tell by the way he put his arm around his wife's shoulder that he worried I might be too much for her, in some way. They'd both grown up in the Midwest, and I'd grown up on the Upper West Side – which was no doubt why Pennsylvania had seemed like Siberia to me in my college days. I'd liked the writer's protectiveness, and I'd picked up on the fact that he wanted his wife to talk to people on her own, but the minute she did, he wanted to make sure she was comfortable. When he saw that we were giggling and talking about jewellery, he'd gone away.

'Anna?' Lucia said. 'You seem to have turned your attention inward. If I didn't know you so well, I might think I'd surprised you.'

'I don't care who you have a relationship with,' I said. 'If you really care what I think about lesbianism, I approve of whatever relationship brings people happiness.'

I walked away, up the aisle. When I was younger, I would have bought into it, assumed I was involved, just because someone older insisted I be. Now, I thought how nice it would be to listen to music I wanted to listen to, instead of the tinkling piano at the hotel. I wouldn't feel I had to offer to pay for my own drink, because I'd already paid earlier in the week, when I bought myself a bottle of Grey Goose I could pour from, into my favourite etched glass I'd bought at a stoop sale in Brooklyn. What would Christine think of me disappearing? Maybe that I was smart. I wondered how Lucia would lead into the subject. By criticizing Christine for being 'anecdotal', then zinging her with an important fact? Lucia was self-important and manipulative, and if Christine didn't know that by now I could mention the obvious, by way of consolation, later.

Outside, I turned the corner and went into my favourite Chinese restaurant. There were only two tables, both taken, so I went to the counter for takeout. 'Anna!' Wang, the waiter, said, turning the paper menu toward him, pencil poised delicately, like a conductor's baton, to circle what I wanted.

'You don't know she wants shrimp fried rice?' his brother, who was now known as James, said. James was taking night classes at NYU and sometimes asked me for help with his homework. 'Once, twice a month she has chicken with broccoli, but tonight she doesn't want that. This is her look when she's in a hurry. In a hurry, always shrimp fried rice.' He smiled a big smile and circled the correct item and handed the piece of paper through the opening into the kitchen. 'Great reading in my course. The poetry of William Butler Yeats. Next time we'll talk,' James said.

Wang had walked away from the counter and was standing at one of the tables, where a customer with his hands folded on top of his violin case on the shiny tabletop seemed to be giving him a bad time about the beer not being cold enough.

When I left, I held the paper bag away from my coat (I always worried I'd stain it). I'd splurged on the coat three years before, a mid-calf cashmere coat I'd resolved I'd take good care of and wear for years. Every time I slipped into it, it felt possible something good could happen.

In my apartment, no husband, no Walter the dog awaited me. Instead of a pet, I had a terrarium with small plastic knights inside, some on horseback, some felled, some still fighting on AstroTurf sprinkled with red nail polish – a gift from a boyfriend who'd been a disaster, though he'd had a great sense of humour. I took off my coat, reached in the pocket, ripped up the receipt for the car and threw it in the trash, so I wouldn't be tempted to do something mean, like send it to Lucia. Christine was still my friend, though I was free of her mother now. I'd been without a family for almost ten years, and I didn't want a replacement, with all the inevitable surprises and secrets. The more I thought about it, the more sure I was that the writer hadn't slept with Lucia's friend, but that Lucia's neighbour/ lover was on the make, and if she couldn't have the writer, she'd decided to move on to Lucia. I was glad he'd thrown a brick through her window, glad she'd had at least a moment of fear, that someone had created a little havoc in her so-well-intentioned Princeton life.

I sipped the vodka, admiring the glass, enjoying the taste. And then – though this is merely anecdotal – I picked up the phone, called information, and asked for Arthur's number in Pennsylvania from an operator who said, 'Please hold,' followed by an automated voice that gave me the number. He still lived in the same place. Imagine that: he was where he'd been all his adult life.

Arthur's wife answered on the second ring. She answered pleasantly, the way people did years ago, when there was no screening of calls, no answering machine to kick in. 'Hello,' she said, and I thought: she is completely, *completely* vulnerable. The winter landscape of the little town outside Pittsburgh where she lived came back to me. the white-out sky; the frozen branches always about to snap. If I hung up, she probably wouldn't even know there was such a thing as hitting *69 to find out who the caller was. Or maybe she would, and she'd call back. Maybe she and I would talk, and become fierce enemies, or even best friends – why not, if neighbours in their sixties became lovers? But that couldn't really happen, because she and I were just two voices on the telephone. I didn't have anything against her. Back then, all I'd had against her was that she had him.

'That necklace,' I said, realizing immediately that I needed to raise my voice and speak clearly. 'The one with the lapis lazuli. I was your husband's student – it doesn't matter who I am. I'm calling to explain. I returned it to you in 1994 because I found it on the floor of his office, and knew it must be yours. He didn't see me pick it up. I was poor, and I wanted to keep it, but I figured it was yours, so I sent it back.'

I hung up, crossed the floor and reached into the terrarium. I bent the knees of one of the warriors and put him back in his saddle, atop a shiny black plastic horse. I slipped a shield over another's head, inadvertently toppling him. I delicately stood the figure upright. I decided against a second vodka.

The phone did not ring. I got into bed, under the duvet, then spread my coat on top, the soft collar touching my chin, as I listened to jazz I wanted to hear, long into the night. When the storm started some time after midnight, I imagined the sleet was hard little notes from a piano way across town that had come to pelt my window, telling me to come out. To come out and play, please. ■

Pay Attention

I can only do what is here. But you
Have an entire congregation of choice,
If you are who they say. The child
Believes you cannot be, just

Doing nothing. I watched, I asked
But also without going very far.
I took care of myself. I took care
Of myself, thinking much too often

I took care of someone else.
Everything feels like payment. In fact
We come into this paying. And you, who are
Nowhere to be found, who make

No noise, who cannot be smelled or tasted,
Wander through with all of us wanting you
At the same time. Oh to be wanted
Like that, for you to pull up a chair

And let your knees touch mine.
For one moment not to answer
The other call, not to look
Past my shoulder when something else moves.

BONFIRE

David Long

In his New England town, when Hawkins was a boy, Independence Day was celebrated by the torching of a bonfire, an immense tower of stacked railroad ties stuffed with tyres. The grown-ups set up canvas lawn chairs on the ancient cinder track or the scrub grass of the ball field, kids horsed around on bikes or edged as close as the volunteer firemen would allow, faces baking, hoping for explosions. An updraught of opaque black smoke shot skyward from the topmost tier, obscuring the last of the twilight. Miles away, you could see it, smell the creosote and incinerated rubber. It would still be smouldering the next morning, a mess of acrid debris, like where a small plane had crashed.

Years later, finished with a post-college internship and employed by a marketing firm on the West Coast, he was invited to a Fourth of July party at a co-worker's apartment fifteen floors up in a high-rise. The city had stewed in crap air all day, but on the balcony where he stood, the onshore breeze seemed fresh, cleansed. He'd been on the job just two months, barely knew anyone, including his host, but was glad to be asked, and glad he'd actually come. The stereo was thumping out Johnny Winter, Little Feat, the Allman Brothers, people were drinking beer, wine coolers, carrying around tiny paper plates. When it was dark, everyone would cluster out here to watch the fireworks over in Los Fuentes. That was the plan.

After a while, the host ambled out, asked how he was faring, was he meeting people, etc.?

I'm good, Hawkins answered, raising his Lucky Lager.

The host lifted the lid of his grill and inspected the coals, frowned at Hawkins, man to man, checked whether his fiancée was watching, then shot two bold spurts of starter fluid at the still-black briquettes. Nothing. He gave another squirt, and the whole bottom of the grill *foomped* into blue flame, flooding the air with sooty fumes reeking of petrochemicals. He clapped the lid down triumphantly, gave Hawkins a chuck on the arm and went inside. Hawkins fled to the far end of the balcony, but not before the smoke whisked him back to the bonfires of his hometown. Already that time seemed irretrievably distant. And what a strange ritual, igniting a humongous blaze in summer and then gaping at it, inhaling all that incredibly toxic . . . but now he noticed a woman on the neighbouring balcony. Slim, olivey, wearing a wrap-around summer dress, tie-dyed rayon or silk. As she stood smoking, gazing off, the breeze swished the hem about her slim, olivey legs. When she caught him looking, she smiled peaceably – it was, after all, a nice evening, a holiday weekend. He smiled back. It seemed like they were fellow passengers at the railing of a ship, first night out.

He looked away.

Then looked back.

All at once, he felt . . . hollowed out, cavernous, *vacant.* A split second later, the way air pounds into the vacuum behind a hurtling tanker truck, he was body-slammed by longing for this woman. Pure uncut desire. Never had he known anything remotely like this, *ever.* It was all he could do to keep his knees from buckling.

Before she could vanish, he motioned for her to come around to where the party was. Good-naturedly, she gestured back. *No, sorry, can't.*

His face went rubbery, but he couldn't take his eyes from her.

She had a last drag on her smoke and spiked it out in a galvanized sand bucket, cleared the hair from her face, twisted it into a ropy shock and held it one-handed, looking at him. Finally, she nodded back toward her apartment, which he took to mean, *Why don't you come over here?*

Next thing, he was plunging his hand into the tubful of melting ice cubes, yanking out two dripping silver cans, making his way into the corridor.

She already had the door half-open.

Hey, she said.

Hey, Hawkins said back.

The apartment was basically empty, he was surprised to see. A few packing cartons, a twin mattress askew on the shag rug beside the air conditioner, a mop, the lingering scent of Mr. Clean.

Before he could ask, she waved her arm at the place. *This was my sister's*, she said. *She had to split for Anchorage, so I'm –*

Hawkins nodded, snapped open a beer, handed it to her, opened his own, drank, watching her drink. She had a wide mouth, eyes the colour of sun tea. His neck went bristly. He felt one step away from the membrane between worlds. Without deliberating, he looked her straight on and said, *I have to tell you something* – and began explaining what had transpired on the balcony, not diluting it, not going, *I know this sounds like total bullshit* – The thing was, she appeared to be listening, attentively, as if they were trying to classify some specimen brought in from the wild.

So how's this different from ordinary lust? she asked.

Ordinary lust? Hawkins said. *Man, I don't know, that doesn't begin to –* He stopped, gathered himself. *It's like ordinary lust is one-dimensional –*

She took this in.

Suddenly she spun around and went toward the kitchen, saying over her shoulder, *Keep talking.*

Hawkins watched her pinch up the remains of a joint from a jar lid, dexterously get it lit, then scoot back and put it to his lips. He willed himself not to cough. It was good for one more each, then she swallowed the roach.

They stood regarding each other.

No, what this is, Hawkins said at last, *is extraordinary lust.* He drew the backs of two fingers along her jaw, slow motion.

Now she walked away again. Going to reset the air conditioner, he guessed, but when she turned, the string ties of the dress were undone, and it was starting to unfurl. She looked surprised to see him way across the room still.

What? she said. *You convinced me. C'mon.*

She shrugged the slippery cloth off her shoulders, let it fall, knelt and smoothed out the one blue sheet.

Hawkins came and stood over her.

You know what? she said. *You should take your pants off. Before they rip.*

Well, it was true, he was scary hard.

A minute or two later, she was straddling him, rocking semi-languidly, droopy-eyeing him. She was uncommonly flat-chested, but he found her sexy beyond words . . . her ribs making a lattice of shadows along the breastbone, her nipples like buffed mahogany in the evening light –

But then he was saying, *Wait, ah* – seizing her forearm, *wait, wait, wait, wait – Don't move. Pretend I'm an unexploded bomb.*

She went dead still. Gingerly, she lowered her face to his. *Count backward from two hundred by elevens,* she whispered.

Hawkins told her they were beyond math.

She gave him a truly sorrowful look, simultaneously flexing muscles he couldn't see.

Stop, no, he said, *I got a plan. Just put me out of my misery . . . then go in the other room and have one slooooow cigarette, and when you come back we can do this as long as you like.*

As long as I like.

Absolutely, Hawkins said. *Hand to my heart.*

But I want to watch.

He gave her a *huh?* look.

The, you know, ka-boom.

Hawkins smiled a bliss-dumb smile.

Then she was rising on to her toes, becoming sort of *airborne* – for a split second they were touching in only one spot. She landed with a little smack.

Oh fucking Jesus – he said, giving her just enough time to take a front-row seat.

Moments of oblivion . . . then he heard her go, *Wow. I've never seen anyone come so much.*

She doodled her finger through a squiggle of it at his collarbone. But suddenly she clutched at him as if stricken. She ducked her head, craned her neck warily and began checking all around on the ceiling, almost keeping a straight face.

Very possibly the funniest thing he'd seen in his entire life.

Anyway, she let him recover for the time it took to have a smoke, maybe two, then moseyed back to bed, and they fucked and fucked and fucked, eventually getting into the shower and lathering each other, then he washed her hair and slowly combed it out as she sat on the rim of the tub, now and then gathering it and lifting it to kiss her neck. At first light, they dressed, rode the elevator down, walked through the placid morning air to a coffee shop, just opening, where they were engulfed by the smell of sweet rolls. Later, in front of her building, they said goodbye. Actually, it took several tries, but finally they parted.

He never saw her again.

At first, he remembered everything – her taste, her beautiful fingers, her hard slender torso, like warm cypress wood, their sex-drunk giggling, the alternating squalls of fatigue and joy. *All of it.* At first, too, those hours with her seemed an omen, a foretaste of what true adult life would hold . . . not unforgettable sex, necessarily, but that a day or night could just crack open and lay adventure at his feet.

Time passed.

Without warning, his company was sold to a conglomerate and most of the local staff was let go. Hawkins scaled back, eventually found another job within commuting distance, but accepted a cut in pay and benefits. Eighteen months later, they transferred him to the Phoenix office. The Phoenix office proved a tense, cut-throat spot – he never truly adjusted to it, never got over his dislike of Phoenix, or the vague belief that he was living, somehow, in exile. At thirty-five, impulsively, he gave up corporate America and went to graduate school . . . winding up in the guidance office of a Portland-area high school, where, as the months accumulated, he came to know the feeling of right livelihood.

Even after he was married and had a family, he still, once in a while, revisited *the night of extraordinary lust*. But now he remembered only what he'd already remembered – it was like shuffling through the same small batch of Polaroids kept in the back of a drawer. Worse, the sweetness hadn't just faded, it had morphed into a form of unease . . . which was maybe on account of working with teenagers all day, but he was riddled with questions: *How could she have been so open? Trusted him? It was insane. And no condoms, no mention of condoms?* But possibly the most unsettling: *How could it have struck them both as reasonable to walk away, to go blithely into separate lives . . . as if the world's largesse had no limit?*

More time went by.

One night, alone in the house – his older daughter at play practice, the younger sleeping over at a friend's, his wife back at her school for parent meetings – Hawkins sits glued to a TV news report from the Middle East: a vast oilfield is burning uncontrollably. Apocalyptic fireballs roil up from well after well, billow into cumulus clouds of pure carbon, obliterating the sky. Half the globe away, he all but smells it, imagines it searing his sinuses, blackening the inside of his skull like the chimney of a kerosene lamp. That quickly he's a boy in his twenties again, inhaling the smoke of a charcoal grill, his watery eyes first lighting on his slender lover-to-be, a life stretching before him. But an altogether different ache blindsides him now, makes him tremble, then convulse with dry sobs.

By the time his wife finds him, he's depleted, hump-shouldered, fist to his mouth. *Hawk*, she says, kneeling, killing the muted TV, *what's wrong? What is it?*

But what can he say? *I'm sad about the world? I'm sad because everything burns?*

She honours his silence a few moments, then leans in and tilts his chin up, two-fingered, until she fills his field of vision.

C'mon, sweetie, she says. *It's been a long one. C'mon upstairs.* She stands, puts both hands out.

Hawkins breathes, takes hold, lets her help him up. ∎

IN SIGHT OF
THE LAKE

Alice Munro

A woman goes to her doctor to have a prescription renewed. But the doctor is not there. It's her day off. In fact the woman has got the day wrong, she has mixed up Monday with Tuesday.

This is the very thing she wanted to talk to the doctor about, as well as renewing the prescription. She has wondered if her mind is slipping a bit.

'What a laugh,' she has expected the doctor to say. 'Your mind. You of all people.'

(It isn't that the doctor knows her all that well, but they do have friends in common.)

Instead, the doctor's assistant phones a day later to say that the prescription is ready and that an appointment has been made for the woman – her name's Jean – to be examined by a specialist about this mind problem.

It isn't mind. It's just memory

Whatever. The specialist deals with elderly patients.

Indeed. Elderly patients who are off their nut.

The girl laughs. Finally, somebody laughs.

She says that the specialist's office is located in a village called Hymen, twenty or so miles away from where Jean lives.

'Oh dear, a marriage specialist,' says Jean.

The girl begs her pardon.

'Never mind. I'll be there.'

What has happened in the last few years is that specialists are located all over the place. Your CAT scan is in one town and your cancer person in another, pulmonary problems in a third, and so on. This is so you won't have to travel to the city hospital, but it can take about as long, since not all these towns have hospitals and you have to ferret out where the doctor is once you get there.

It is for this reason that Jean decides to drive to the village of the Elderly Specialist – as it seems suitable to call him – on the evening before the day of her appointment. That should give her lots of time to find out where he is, so there will be no danger of her arriving all flustered or even a little late and creating a bad impression right off the bat.

Her husband asks if she would like him to go with her, but she knows that he wants to watch a soccer game on television. He is a poet who watches sports half the night and makes up poetry the other half, though he tells her to say he is retired.

She says she wants to find the place herself. The girl in the doctor's office has given her directions.

The evening is beautiful. But when she turns off the highway, driving west, she finds that the sun is just low enough to shine into her face. If she sits up quite straight, however, and lifts her chin, she can get her eyes above the blind ahead. Also, she has good sunglasses. She can read the sign, which tells her that she has eight miles to go to the village of Highman.

Highman. Population 1,553.

Why do they bother to put the 3 on?

Every soul counts.

She has a habit of checking out small places, to see if she could live there. This one seems to fit the bill. A decent-sized market, where you could get fairly fresh vegetables, though they would not often be from the fields roundabout, OK coffee. Then a laundromat and a pharmacy, which could fill your prescriptions even if they didn't stock the better class of magazines.

There were signs of course that the place had seen better times. A clock that no longer told the time presided over a window that promised Fine Jewellery but now appeared to be full of any old china, crocks and pails and wreaths twisted out of wires.

She could make out some of the doctor's trash because the space in the front of this forsaken shop was where he had chosen to park. She felt like looking for his office on foot. And almost too soon to give her satisfaction she saw a dark brick one-storey building in the utilitarian style of the last century and she could bet that was it. Doctors in small towns like this used to have their working quarters as part of their houses, then they had to have more space where cars could park, and they put up something like this. Reddish-brown bricks, and sure enough the sign, Medical Dental. A parking lot behind it.

In her pocket she has the doctor's name and she gets out the scrap of paper to check it. The names on the frosted-glass door are Dr H.W. Forsyth, Dentist, and Dr Donald McMillen, Physician.

These names are not on Jean's piece of paper. And no wonder, because nothing is written there but a number. It is the shoe size of her husband's sister, who is dead. The number is O – 7½. It takes her a while to figure that out, the O standing for Olivia but scribbled in that hasty way, and even then she can only recall faintly something about getting slippers when Olivia was in the hospital.

That's no use to her anyway.

One solution is that the doctor she will see has newly moved into this building and the name on the door has not been changed yet. She should ask somebody. First she should ring the bell on the off chance that somebody is in there, working late. She does this, and it is a good thing in a way that nobody comes, because the doctor's name that she is after has still not risen to the surface of her mind.

Another idea. Isn't it quite possible that this person – the crazy-doctor, as she has chosen to call him, when speaking to her husband – isn't it quite possible that he (or she – like most people of her age she does not automatically allow for that possibility) – that he or she does operate out of a house? It would make sense and be cheaper. You don't need a lot of apparatus for the crazy-doctoring.

So she continues her walk away from the main street. The houses she walks by were mostly built in the nineteenth century. Some of wood, some of brick. The brick ones often two full storeys high, the wooden ones somewhat more modest, a storey and a half with slanting ceilings in the upstairs rooms. Some front doors opened just a few feet from the sidewalk. Others on to wide verandas, occasionally glassed-in. A century ago, on an evening like this one, people would have been sitting on their verandas or perhaps on the front steps. Housewives who had finished washing the dishes and sweeping up the kitchen floors for the last time that day, men who had coiled up the hose after giving the grass a soaking. No garden furniture such as sat here empty, just the wooden steps or dragged-out kitchen chairs. Conversation about the weather or a runaway horse or some person who had taken to bed and was not expected to recover. Speculation about herself, once she was out of earshot. But wouldn't she have put their minds at ease, stopping and asking them please, can you tell me, where is the doctor's house?

New item of conversation. What does she want the doctor for? Once she was out of earshot.

Now they were all inside with their fans on or their air conditioning. Numbers on the houses, just as in a city. No sign of a doctor.

Where the sidewalk ended there was a large brick building with gables and a clock tower. Perhaps a school, before the children were bussed to some larger and drearier centre of learning. The hands stopped at twelve, for noon or midnight, which certainly was not the right time. Profusion of summer flowers that seemed professionally arranged – some spilling out of a wheelbarrow and more out of a milk pail on its side. A sign she could not read because the sun was shining straight into it. She climbed up on to the lawn to see it at another angle.

Funeral Home. Now she saw the built-on garage that must hold the hearse, and some built-on businesslike addition that could have been for a swimming pool or indoor badminton court. But in this case wasn't.

She turned on to a side street where there was no sidewalk. Less well-kept houses, a frank lot of clutter out in front. But after a block or so a surprise. Very well-kept places indeed, so that the town or village became a suburb, the houses all slightly different yet somehow looking all the same. Gently coloured stone or pale brick, peaked or rounded windows, a rejection of the utilitarian look, the ranch style of past decades.

To her eyes they looked a little silly.

Nevertheless there were people out. They hadn't all managed to shut themselves up with the air conditioning. A boy was riding a bicycle, taking diagonal routes across the pavement. Something about his riding was odd, and she could not figure it out at first.

He was riding backwards. A jacket flung in such a way that you could not see – or she could not see – what was wrong.

A woman who might have been too old to be his mother – but was very trim and lively-looking all the same – was standing out in the street watching him. She was holding on to a skipping rope and talking to a man who could not have been her husband – both of them were being too cordial.

The street was a curved dead end. There was no use going further.

Interrupting the adults, Jean excused herself. She said that she was looking for a doctor.

'No, no,' she said. 'Don't be alarmed. Just his address. I thought you might know.'

Then came the problem of explaining that she was not sure of the name. They were too polite to show any surprise at this but they could not help her.

The boy on one of his perverse sallies came swinging around, barely missing all three.

Laughter. No reprimand. They all remarked on the beauty of the evening, and Jean turned to go back the way that she had come.

Except that she did not go all the way, not as far as the Funeral Home. There was a side street she had ignored before, perhaps because it was unpaved and she had not thought of a doctor living in such circumstances.

There was no sidewalk, and the houses looked to have not much relationship to each other. A couple of men were busy under the hood of a truck, but she thought it would not do to interrupt them. Besides, she has glimpsed something interesting ahead.

There is a hedge that comes right out to the street. It is high enough that she does not expect to be able to see around it, but thinks she might be able to peek through.

That is not necessary. The lot – about the size of four town lots, really – is quite open to the road she is walking on. There appeared to be some sort of park, with flagstone paths diagonally crossing the mown and flourishing green grass. In between the paths, and bursting from the grass, there were flowers. She knows some of them – the dark gold and light yellow daisies for instance, pink and rosy and red-hearted white phlox – but she is no great gardener herself and there are clumps of all colours that she could not name. Some climbed trellises, some spread free. Everything artful but nothing stiff, not even the fountain that shot up seven feet or so before falling down into its rock-lined pool. She has walked in off the street to get a little of its cool spray, and there she finds a wrought-iron bench, where she can sit down.

A man has come along one of the paths, carrying a pair of shears. Gardeners evidently expected to work late here.

It has not occurred to her that this could be anything but a town park.

Tall and very thin and dressed in black shirt and pants that closely fitted his body.

'This is really beautiful,' she called to him, quite sincerely yet in her most assured and ladylike, almost beguiling voice. 'You keep it up so well.'

'Thank you,' he said. 'You're welcome to rest there.'

Informing her by some dryness of voice that this was not a park but private property, and that he was not a village employee but the owner.

'I should have asked your permission.'

'That's OK.'

Preoccupied, bending and snipping at a plant that was encroaching on the path.

'It's yours, is it? All of it?'

After a moment's business, 'All of it.'

'I should have known. It's too imaginative to be public. Too unusual.'

No answer. She was going to ask him whether he liked to sit here by himself, in the evenings. But she would not bother. He was not an easy person to be around. One of those who prided himself, probably, on being like that. After a moment she would thank him and get up.

But after a moment he came and sat down beside her. He spoke just as if the question had been put to him.

'Actually I only feel comfortable when I'm doing something that needs attending to,' he said. 'If I sit down I have to keep my eyes off everything, or I'll just see some more work.'

She should have seen right away that he was a man who didn't like banter. But still she was curious.

What was here before?

Before he made the garden?

'A knitting factory. All these little places had something like that; you could get away with the starvation wages. But in time that went under and there was a contractor who thought he was going to turn it into a nursing home. There was some trouble then, the town wouldn't give him a licence, they had some idea there'd be a lot of old people around and they'd make it depressing. So he set fire to it or he knocked it down, I don't know.'

He's not from around here, she thought, or he wouldn't talk so openly.

'I'm not from around here,' he said. 'I don't know everything. But I had a friend who was from here and when he died I came and I was just going to get rid of his house and go. His house is over there.'

She could see now beyond a mountain-ash tree a house that didn't look as if it could have anything to do with this garden.

'Then I got hold of this cheap because the contractor had left it just a hole in the ground and it was an eyesore.'

'I'm sorry to be so inquisitive.'

'That's all right. If I don't feel like telling I don't answer.'

'I haven't been here before,' she said. 'Of course I haven't, or I would have seen this spot. I was walking around looking for something. I thought I could find it better if I parked my car and just walked. I was looking for a certain doctor's office, actually.'

She explains about not being sick, just having an appointment tomorrow, and not wanting to be running around then looking for the place. Then about parking her car and being surprised that the name of the doctor she wanted was not listed there.

'I couldn't look in the phone book either because you know how the phone books and the payphones have all disappeared now. Or else you find their insides ripped out anyway. Of course you would often find the phone book ripped away.'

'It's so silly.'

She tries again to think of the name but he says it wouldn't ring a bell anyway.

'But I don't go to doctors.'

'You're probably smart not to.'

'Oh, I wouldn't say that.'

'At any rate, I'd better get back to my car.'

Standing up when she did, he says he will walk with her.

'So I won't get lost.' She means it as some mild sort of joke relating to her fecklessness so far.

'I always try to stretch my legs at this time of the evening. Working in the garden is OK but it can leave you cramped.'

'I'm sure there's some sensible explanation. I must strike you as some crazy old biddy not fit to be let out alone.'

The garden is a memorial to the friend who died. Gay. Lovers.

How she would like to talk to somebody fresh.

They walked along without meeting a soul. Soon they reached the main street, with the medical building just a block away. For some reason the sight of it made her feel shaky, and absurdly alarmed lest the right name should have been in place all the time, and she had just managed to miss it. She left his side when they got to it, saw that she had not been mistaken, and then pretended that her interest had been all the time in the next window with its strange assortment of china-headed dolls and ancient skates and chamber pots and quilts already in tatters.

'Isn't this peculiar?' she said. 'I mean, can you think of anybody –'

He was not paying attention to her. He said that he had just thought of something.

'This doctor,' he said.

'Yes?'

'I wonder if he might be connected with the Home?'

They were walking again, passing a couple of young men sitting on the sidewalk, one with his legs stretched out. He took no notice of them, but his voice had dropped.

'Home?' she said.

'You wouldn't have noticed if you came in from the highway. But if you keep going out of town towards the lake you pass it. Not more than half a mile out. You go past the gravel pile on the south side of the road and it's just a little further on, on the other side. I don't know if they have a live-in doctor there or not but it stands to reason they might have.'

'They might have,' she copied him, and then wondered why on earth she had done it. 'It stands to reason.' She wanted to go on talking to him longer, to begin making silly jokes. But she had to think about the whereabouts of her keys, as she often did before getting into the car. She was regularly worried about whether she'd locked the keys inside or dropped them somewhere. She could feel the approach of familiar, tiresome panic, then she found them, in her pocket.

'It's worth a try,' he said and she agreed, thanking him.

'There's plenty of room to turn off the road and take a look. If there's a doctor out there regularly, there's no need for him to have his name up in town. Or her name, as the case might be.'

As if he, too, was not anxious for them to part.

'I have you to thank,' she said.

'Just a hunch.'

He held the door and closed it, and waited there until she had turned to go in the right direction, then waved goodbye.

When she was on her way out of the town she caught sight of him again in the rear-view mirror. He was bending over, speaking to a couple of boys or young men who were sitting on the pavement with their backs against the wall of the store. They had been there when he was with her but he had not bothered with them.

Maybe a remark to be made, some joke about her vagueness or silliness. Or just her.

She had thought that she would come back through the village and thank him again and tell him the doctor's name (she was pretty certain now that she would find it). She could just slow down and laugh and call it out the window.

But now she thought that she should just take the lake shore, and stay out of his way.

Never mind. She saw the gravel pile coming up, she had to pay attention to where she was going.

Just as he had said. A sign. A notice of the Lakeview Rest Home. And there really was, from here, a view of the lake, a thread of pale blue along the horizon.

A spacious parking lot. One long wing with what looked like separate compartments or good-sized rooms, at least, with their own little gardens or places to sit in front of them. A latticed fence quite high in front of every one of them for privacy or safety. Though nobody was sitting out there that she could see.

Of course bedtime came early in these establishments.

She liked how the latticework would provide a touch of fantasy.

The main wing, where the front door was, had a more serious or official style. Public buildings had been changing in the past few years, just as private houses had. The relentless, charmless look, the only one permitted in her youth, had disappeared. Here she parked in front of a bright dome that had a look of welcome, of cheerful excess. Some people would find it fakey, she supposed, but wasn't it the very thing you would want? All that glass must cheer the spirits of the old people, or even, perhaps, of some of the deranged people who had to be lodged here.

She looked for a button to push, a bell to ring, as she walked up to the door. But it was not necessary – the door opened on its own. And once you got inside there was an even greater expression of space, of loftiness, a blue tinge to the glass. The floor was all silvery tiles, the sort that children loved to slide upon, and for a moment the thought of these people sliding and slipping made her happy. Of course it couldn't be as slippery as it looked, you would not want them breaking their necks.

'I didn't dare try it myself,' she said to somebody in her head. 'It wouldn't have done, would it? I could have found myself in front of the doctor who was going to test my mental stability.'

At the moment there was no doctor to be seen.

Well, there wouldn't be. Doctors didn't sit behind desks here waiting for patients to show up, did they?

And she wasn't even here for a consultation, just checking up on an elusive name, and making sure of the time she was to show up tomorrow.

There was a rounded desk, waist-high, whose panels of dark wood looked like mahogany though they probably weren't. Nobody behind it at the moment. It was after hours of course. She looked for a bell but did not see one. Then she looked to see if there was a list of doctors' names or even one name of a doctor in charge. She did not see that either. You would think there would be a way of getting hold of somebody, no matter what the hour. Somebody on call in a place like this.

No important clutter behind the desk, either. No computer or telephone or papers or coloured buttons to press. Of course she wasn't able to get right behind, there seemed to be some lock, so there might be compartments she could not see. Buttons a receptionist could get at and you couldn't.

She gave up on the desk for the moment, and took a close look at the space she found herself in. It was a hexagon, with doors at intervals. Four doors – one was the large door that let in the light and any visitors, another an official and private-looking door behind the desk, not that easy to access, and the other two doors, exactly alike and facing each other, would obviously take you into the long wings, to the corridors and rooms where the inmates were housed. Each of these had an upper window, and the window glass looked frank and clear enough for anybody to manage.

She went up to one of these possibly accessible doors and knocked, then tried the knob and could not budge it. Locked. She could not see through the window properly, either. Close up, the glass was all distorted.

In the door directly opposite there was the same problem with the glass and the same problem with the knob.

The click of her shoes on the floor, the trick of the glass, the uselessness of the polished knobs made her feel slightly more discouraged than she would care to show.

She didn't give up, however. She tried the doors again in the same order, and this time she shook both knobs as well as she could and also called out, 'Hello?' in a voice that sounded at first weak and silly, then aggrieved, but no more hopeful.

She squeezed herself in behind the desk and banged that door, with practically no hope. It did not even have a knob, just a keyhole. There was nothing to do but get out of this place and go home.

All very cheerful and elegant, she thought, but there was no pretence here of serving the public. Of course they shoved the residents or patients or whatever they called them into bed early, it was the same story however glamorous the surroundings.

Still thinking about this, she gave the big door a push. It was too heavy. She pushed again.

Again. It did not budge.

Again, again. She could see the pots of flowers. Outside a car going by on the road. The mild evening light.

She had to stop and think.

There were no artificial lights on in here. The place would get dark. Already in spite of the lingering light outside, it seemed to be getting dark. No one would come, they had all completed their duties, or at least the duties that brought them through this part of the building.

She opened her mouth to scream but it seemed that no scream was forthcoming. She was shaking all over and no matter how she tried she could not get her breath down into her lungs. It was just as if she had a blotter in her throat. Suffocation. She knew that she had to behave differently, and more than that, to believe differently. Calm. Calm. Breathe. Breathe. She knew the right thing but her mind was swamped, her head was swamped with blackness. Thick. Not air any more. Nothing available to her but a head of wool.

Better,' she said. 'Oh, what a relief. To be better.' The person with her was wearing a blue-flowered smock and plain blue pants. Her name was Sandy – it said so on a pretty sequinned pin on her shoulder. Aside from that there was nothing about her that indicated an interest in decoration. She was heavy and plain and probably younger than she looked. A bunch of kids at home. A slack husband, if any.

She said, 'OK, Jean.'

'It is such a relief,' Jean said. 'I'll just tell you briefly what I have been bothering around about and then I have to get home. It's extraordinary what I've been through for such a simple thing. You see, I have an appointment to see a doctor whose name I can't seem to get straight but I was supposed to find him here and I have followed some directions as well as I could but no luck. I felt that I'd got into some ridiculous sort of trap and I must have a tendency to be claustrophobic, it was alarming –'

'Oh, Jean, hurry up,' said Sandy. 'I'm behind already and I have to get you into your nightie and all. That's the same thing you tell me every time.' ∎

Twelve Minutes of Love: A Tango Story
Kapka Kassabova

To the uninitiated, tango is just a dance. To the true *tanguero*,
it is something akin to a religion. Here, in spring-heeled prose,
Kassabova takes us inside the esoteric world of tango to tell the story
of the dance. *Twelve Minutes of Love* is a timeless tale of exile and
longing, love and belonging, which confirms Kassabova as one of
the most dazzling writers of her generation.
Portobello Books £18.99 | HB

The Third Reich *Roberto Bolaño*

The discovery, after his death, of a masterpiece by Roberto Bolaño
is a major literary event. Combining the exhilaration of *The Savage
Detectives* with the dark brilliance of *2666* in a visceral book exploring
memory, madness and violence, *The Third Reich* is both the perfect way
to discover the genius of Roberto Bolaño and an unmissable addition to
the oeuvre for those who already have.
Picador

Ambit Edited by *Martin Bax*

The quarterly magazine that publishes poetry, prose and artwork,
Ambit celebrated its 50th birthday in 2010 and is still going
strong. Ingrid Bergman, Bob Dylan, Charles Bukowski and *Alice in
Wonderland* are to be found wandering through the pages of *Ambit*
206, in which Geoff Nicholson asks the big questions, Gerda Mayer
recalls love in a time of war, and Joan Jobe Smith go-go dances in LA.
www.ambitmagazine.co.uk
Ambit £9

American Dervish *Ayad Akhtar*

A stirring and explosive debut novel about an American Muslim
family's struggle with faith and belonging, from acclaimed screen-
writer Ayad Akhtar.
Weidenfeld & Nicolson £12.99 | HB

THE END?

John Barth

In 2011 and 2012, two new products of this pen – a novel entitled *Every Third Thought* and an essay collection entitled *Final Fridays* – are scheduled for publication. Both were completed in 2009, my eightieth year of life and fifty-third as a publishing writer. At the time of their composition I didn't think of them as my *last* books, only as the latest. But in the time since, although I've still gone to my workroom every weekday morning for the hours between breakfast and lunch, as I've done for decades, and faithfully re-enacted my muse-inviting ritual, I find that I've written . . . nothing.

That room is divided into three distinct areas: COMPOSITION (one side of a large worktable, reserved for longhand first drafts of fiction on Mondays through Thursdays and non-fiction on Fridays, with supply drawers and adjacent reference-book shelves), PRODUCTION (computer hutch with desktop word processor and printer for subsequent drafts and revision), and BUSINESS (other side of worktable, with desk calendar and office files). As for the ritual:

Step One is to seat myself at the Composition table, set down my refilled thermal mug of breakfast coffee and insert the wax earplugs that I got in the habit of using back in the 1950s, when my three children (now in *their* fifties) were rambunctious toddlers, and that became so associated with my sentence-making that even as a long-time empty-nester in a quiet house, I continue to feel the need for them.

Step Two is to open the stained and battered three-ring loose-leaf binder, now sixty-three years old and held precariously together with strapping tape, that I bought during my freshman orientation week at Johns Hopkins in 1947 and in which I penned all my undergraduate and grad-school class notes, professorial lecture drafts during my decades in academia, and first drafts of the entire corpus of my fiction and non-fiction.

Step Three is to unclip from that binder's middle ring the British Parker 51 fountain pen bought during my maiden tour of Europe in 1963–4 (in a Volkswagen camper with those same three then small children and their mother) at a Rochester stationer's alleged to be the original of Mister Pumblechook's premises in Dickens's *Great Expectations*: the pen with which I have penned every subsequent sentence, including this one. (Its predecessor, an also much-valued Sheaffer that saw me through college and my first three published novels, was inadvertently cracked in my shirt pocket a few weeks earlier when I leaned against a battlement in 'Hamlet's castle' in 'Elsinore' – Danish Helsingør, near Copenhagen, the northernmost stop of that makeshift Grand Tour – in order to get a better view of Sweden across the water.) I recharge the venerable Parker with jet-black Quink, wipe its well-worn tip with a bit of tissue, fix its cap on to its butt, and proceed to Step Four . . .

Which in happier days meant reviewing and editing either the printouts of yesterday's first-draft pages (left off when the going was good and thus more readily resumed) or work notes toward some project in gestation, to be followed by Step Five: re-inspiration and the composition of new sentences, paragraphs and pages. Of late, however, Step Four has consisted of staring vainly, pen in hand, at blank ruled pages, or exchanging fountain pen for note-taking ballpoint and perusing for possible suggestions either my spiral-bound Work Notebook #5 (*2008–*) or my little black six-ring loose-leaf personal notebook/diary, to no avail. That latter has only a few blank leaves remaining, and no room for more. And the workroom's bookshelves, reserved for one copy of each edition and translation of every book, magazine article and anthology contribution that I've perpetrated, are already crowded beyond their capacity, with new editions lying horizontally across older ones and jammed into crannies between bookcase and wall.

That almost-exhausted notebook-space, those overflowing shelves – are they trying to tell me something? I plug my ears; strain not to listen. Like most fiction writers of my acquaintance (perhaps especially those who mainly write novels rather than short stories), I'm accustomed to a well-filling interval of some weeks or even months between book-length projects: an interval not to be confused with 'writer's block'. Indeed, I've learned to look forward to that bit of respite from sentence-making after a new book has left the shop – bulky typescript both snail-mailed and emailed to agent and thence to publisher – and to busily making notes toward the Next One while final copy-editing and galley proofing its predecessor. This time, however . . .

Well.

Well? A writer-friend from Kansas who knows about water-wells informs me of the important distinction between *dry* wells and 'gurglers', which may cease producing for a time but eventually resume; he encourages me to believe that I am, if no longer a geyser, still a gurgler, not yet a mere geezer. May that prove to be the case – but if in fact the well is dry, I remind myself that as we've aged, my wife and I have been obliged to put other much enjoyed pleasures behind us: snow- and waterskiing, tennis, sailboat cruising on the Chesapeake and, yes, even vigorous youthful sex (but certainly not love and intimacy, and as someone once wisely observed, 'Sex goes; memory goes; but the memory of sex – that never goes'). If my vocation – my 'calling'! – turns out to have joined that sigh-and-smile list of Once Upon a Times, its memory will be a cherished one indeed.

Time will tell.

Meanwhile, maybe write a little piece about . . . not writing? ∎

NOTICEBOARD

GRANTA

WAR DOGS

Aleksandar Hemon

Tina and Mek. Sarajevo, 1991
Courtesy Aleksandar Hemon

My family's first and only dog arrived in the spring of 1991. That April, my sister drove with her new boyfriend to Novi Sad, a town in northern Serbia hundreds of miles from Sarajevo, where there was an Irish-setter breeder she'd somehow tracked down. In her early twenties, my sister was still living with our parents, but she'd long asserted her unimpeachable right to do whatever she felt like. Thus, without even consulting Mama and Tata, with the money she'd saved from her modelling gigs, she bought a gorgeous, blazingly auburn Irish-setter puppy. When she brought him home, Tata was shocked – city dogs were self-evidently useless, a resplendent Irish setter even more so – and unconvincingly demanded that she return him immediately. Mama offered some predictable rhetorical resistance to yet another creature (after a couple of cats she'd had to mourn) she would worry about excessively, but it was clear she fell in love with the dog on the spot. Within a day or two he chewed up someone's shoe and was instantly forgiven. We named him Mek.

In a small city like Sarajevo, where people are tightly interconnected and no one can live in isolation, all experiences end up shared. Just as Mek joined our family, my best friend Veba, who lived across the street from us, acquired a dog himself, a German shepherd named Don. Čika-Vlado, Veba's father, a low-ranking officer of the Yugoslav People's Army, was working at a military warehouse near Sarajevo where a guard dog gave birth to a litter of puppies. Veba drove over to his father's workplace and picked the slowest, clumsiest puppy, as he knew that, if they were to be destroyed, that one would be the first one to go.

Veba had been my sister's first boyfriend and the only one I'd ever really liked. We were often inseparable, particularly after we'd started making music and playing in a band together. After my sister managed to get over their break-up, they renewed their friendship. Soon after the puppies arrived, they'd take them out for a walk at the same time. I was no longer living with my parents, but often came home for food and family time, particularly after Mek's arrival – I loved to take him out, my childhood dream of owning a pet fulfilled by my indomitable sister. Veba and I would walk with Mek and Don by the river, or sit on a bench and watch them roll in the grass, smoking and talking about music and books, girls and movies, while our dogs gnawed playfully at each other's throats. I don't know how dogs really become friends, but Mek and Don were as close friends as Veba and I were.

Much of the summer of 1991 I spent in Kiev, Ukraine, managing to be present for the demise of the Soviet Union and Ukraine's declaration of independence. That same summer, the war in Croatia progressed rapidly from incidents to massacres, from skirmishes to the Yugoslav People's Army's completely destroying the town called Vukovar. When I returned from Ukraine at the end of August, there was not fighting yet in Sarajevo – the siege would commence the following spring – but the war had already settled in people's minds: fear, confusion and drugs reigned. I had no money, so a friend of mine offered me hack work on a porn magazine (he thought that people would want distraction from the oncoming disaster), but I declined, because I didn't want bad sex writing (as though there were any other kind) to be the last thing I'd done if I were to be killed in the war. I packed a carful of books and moved up to our cabin on a mountain called Jahorina to read as many thick classical novels as possible (and write a slim volume of muddled stories) before the war consigned everything and all to death and oblivion. If I was going down, I was going down reading (and writing).

I stayed in the mountains from September to December. I read the fat classics (*War and Peace*, *The Magic Mountain*) and Kafka's letters; I wrote stuff full of madness, death and wordplay; I listened to music while staring at the embers in our fireplace; I chopped wood.

At night, I could hear the tree branches over our cabin scratching the roof in the wind; the wooden frame creaked and, occasionally, the bell of a lost cow echoed through the dense night. Years later, I would struggle to perform exercises that were supposed to help me with managing my frequent outbursts of anger. On the advice of my therapist, I'd try to control my breathing while envisioning in detail a place I associated with peace and safety. I'd invariably invoke our cabin in the mountains: the smooth surface of the wooden table my father built without using a single nail; a cluster of old ski passes hanging under the mute cuckoo clock; the ancient fridge whose brand name – *Obod Cetinje* – were the first words I read by myself. The peace and safety belonged to the time I'd spent in the cabin, when reading in solitude cleared my mind and my hurt was healed by the crisp mountain air and ubiquitous pine smell.

Mek would also feature prominently in my anger-management visualizations. My parents and sister occasionally gave him leave to keep me company in the mountains. Before sleep, his steady breathing would calm me, distracting me from the cacophony of night sounds. In the early morning, his long warm tongue would wake me up, pasting my face with his happy saliva. He'd put his head in my lap as I read and I'd scratch him behind his ears. I'd go out hiking with him by my side, the thoughts generated by what I'd been reading racing in my head, just as Mek raced up and down the mountain slopes. When Veba came to visit me, we hiked together, while Mek and Don chased each other, stopping only to try to excavate phantom subterranean rodents. We fantasized that, when the war came to Sarajevo, we could always retreat with our dogs to Jahorina and stay up here until it was all over.

The last time we went up to the mountains was to mark the arrival of 1992 – we didn't know then that the week we spent together would amount to a farewell party to our common Sarajevo life. Apart from my sister and me and our friends – ten humans in total – there were also three dogs: Mek, Don and our friend Guša's Laki, an energetic dog of indeterminate breed (Guša called him a cocktail spaniel). In the restricted space of a smallish mountain cabin, the humans would trip over the dogs, while they'd often get into their canine arguments and would have to be pulled apart. One night, playing cards into the wee hours, Guša and I got into a chest-thumping argument, which made the dogs crazy – there was enough barking and screaming to blow the roof off, but I recall that moment with warmth, for all the intense intimacy of our shared previous life was in it.

A couple of weeks later, I departed for the US, never to return to our mountain cabin.

My sister and Veba remember the last time they took Mek and Don for a walk before the war started. It was April 1992, and there was shooting up in the hills around Sarajevo; a Yugoslav People's Army plane menacingly broke the sound barrier above the city; the dogs barked like crazy. They said: 'See you later!' to each other as they parted, but would not see each other for five years.

Soon thereafter, my sister followed her latest boyfriend to Belgrade. My parents stayed behind for a couple of weeks, during which time sporadic gunfire and shelling increased daily. I'd call from Chicago and ask how things were and my mother would say: 'They're already shooting less than yesterday.' More and more, they spent time with their neighbours in the improvised basement shelter. On 2 May 1992, with Mek in tow, Mama and Tata took a train out of Sarajevo before the relentless siege commenced – indeed, half an hour after the train left, the station was subject to a rocket attack; no other train would leave the city for ten years or so.

My parents were heading to the village in north-western Bosnia where my father was born, a few miles from the town of Prnjavor, which came under Serb control. My dead grandparents' house still stood on a hill called Vučijak (translatable as 'Wolfhill'). My father had been keeping beehives on my grandparents' homestead and insisted on leaving Sarajevo largely because it was time to attend to the bees and prepare them for the summer. In wilful denial of the distinct possibility that they might not return for a long time, they brought no warm clothes or passports, just a small bag of summer clothes. All they had was left in Sarajevo.

They spent the first few months of the war on Vučijak, their chief means of sustenance my father's bee-keeping and my mother's vegetable garden. Convoys of drunken Serbian soldiers passed by the house on their way to an ethnic cleansing operation or returning from the front line where they fought the Bosnian forces, singing songs of slaughter or angrily shooting in the air. When the air was clear, my parents, cowering in the house, secretly listened to the news from the besieged Sarajevo. Mek would sometimes happily chase after the military trucks and my parents desperately ran after him, calling out, terrified that the drunken soldiers might shoot him for malicious fun.

Sometime that summer, Mek fell ill. He could not get up on his feet; he refused food and water, there was blood in his urine. My parents laid him on the floor in the bathroom, which was the coolest space in the house – where there was no air conditioning and meals were cooked on a wood stove. My mother would stroke Mek, talking to him, while he looked straight into her eyes – she always claimed he understood everything she told him. They called the vet, but the vet station had only one car at its disposal, which was continuously on the road with the vet on call attending to all the sick animals in the area. It took a couple of days before a vet finally came by. He instantly recognized that Mek was riddled with deer ticks, all of them bloated with his blood, poisoning him. The prognosis was not good, he said, but at the vet station he could give him a shot that might help. My father borrowed my uncle's tractor and cart in which pigs were normally transported to market or slaughter. He put the limp Mek in the cart and drove down the hill, all the way to Prnjavor, to get the shot that could save his life. On his way, he was passed by the Serb Army trucks, the soldiers looking down on the panting Mek.

The magic injection worked and Mek lived, recovering after a few days. But then it was my mother's turn to get terribly sick. Her gall bladder was infected, as it was full of stones – back in Sarajevo, she'd been advised to undergo surgery to remove them, but she'd kept postponing her decision and then the war broke out. Now, her brother, my uncle Milisav, drove down from Subotica, a town at the Serbian–Hungarian border, and took her back with him for urgent surgical treatment. My father had to wait for his friend Dragan to come and get Mek and him. While my father was preparing his beehives for his long absence, Mek would lie nearby, stretched in the grass, keeping him company.

A few days after Mama's departure, Tata's friend Dragan arrived. On the way to get my father, he was stopped at the checkpoint at the top of Vučijak. The men at the checkpoint were drunk and impatient. They asked Dragan where he was heading, and when he told them my father was waiting for him, they menacingly informed him that they'd been watching my father closely for a while, that they knew all about him (my father's family was ethnically Ukrainian – earlier that year the Ukrainian church in Prnjavor had been blown up by the Serbs), and that they were well aware of his son (of me, that is) who had written against the Serbs and was now in America. They were just about ready to take care of my father once and for all, they told Dragan. The men belonged to a paramilitary unit that called itself Vukovi (the Wolves) and were led by one Veljko, whom a few years earlier my father had thrown out of a meeting he'd organized to discuss bringing in running water from a nearby mountain well. Veljko went on to Austria to pursue a rewarding criminal career, only to return right before the war to put his paramilitary unit together. 'You let Hemon know we're coming,' the Wolves told Dragan as they let him through.

When Dragan reported the incident, which he took very seriously, my father thought it would be better to try to get out as soon as possible rather than waiting for the Wolves to come at night and slit his throat. When they drove up the road to the checkpoint, the guard shift had just changed and the new men were not drunk or churlish enough to care, so my father and Dragan were waved through. The Wolves at the checkpoint failed to sniff out or see Mek, because Tata kept him down on the floor. Later on, in their mindless rage, or possibly trying to steal the honey, the Wolves destroyed my father's hives. In a letter he'd send me in Chicago he'd tell me that of all the losses the war inflicted upon him, losing his bees was the most painful.

On their way toward the Serbian border, Tata and Dragan passed many checkpoints. My father was concerned that if those manning the checkpoints saw a beautiful Irish setter, they'd immediately understand that he was coming from a city, as there were few auburn Irish setters in the Bosnian countryside largely populated by mangy mutts and wolves. Furthermore, the armed men could easily get pissed at someone trying to save a fancy dog in the middle of a war, when people were killed left and right. At each checkpoint, Mek would try to get up and my father would press him down with his hand, whispering calming words into his ear. Mek would lie back down. He never produced a sound, never insisted on standing up, and, miraculously, no one at the checkpoints noticed him. My father and Dragan made it out across the border and on to Subotica.

Meanwhile, in Sarajevo under siege, Veba was a conscript in the Bosnian Army defending the city from the units of the former Yugoslav People's Army, now transformed overnight into the genocidal Serb Army. Veba's father, on the other hand, was on duty at his warehouse outside Sarajevo when the hostilities began. As a low-ranking YPA officer, he was expendable enough to be left behind while the Serb units were being redeployed to besiege the city and was taken as a POW by the Bosnian forces soon after the fighting began. Veba and his family would have no news from him for the next few years, not knowing whether he was alive or dead.

While my family was scattered all over elsewhere, Veba's still lived across the street from our home. He was sharing a small apartment with his girlfriend, mother, brother and Don. Very quickly, food became scarce – a good dinner under siege was a slice of bread sprinkled with oil; rice was all that was available for most of the people, meal after meal, day after day. People had nothing to feed a dog with, so packs of abandoned dogs roamed the city, sometimes attacking humans or tearing up fresh corpses. To have and feed a dog was a suspicious luxury, yet Veba's family shared with Don whatever they had. Frequently, there was nothing to share and Don somehow understood the difficulty of the situation and never begged. During shelling, he'd pace around their apartment, sniffing and squealing. He'd become calm only when all of the family were in the same room, whereupon he'd lie down and watch them all closely. If the shelling lasted and he could not be taken out for long stretches of time, he'd always patiently wait. Every once in a while, they'd entertain him by asking: 'Where is Mek? Where is Mek?' and Don would run to the front door and bark excitedly, remembering his friend.

When they took him out, Veba and his family had to stay within a narrow space protected from the Serb snipers and mortar shells by their high-rise. Many of their neighbours admired Don's loyalty and good nature in the middle of a horrible war. The children played with him and he let them pet him. Within weeks, Don developed an uncanny ability to sense an imminent mortar-shell attack: he'd bark and move anxiously in circles; bristling, he'd jump up on Veba's mother's shoulders and push her until she and everyone else rushed back into the building. A moment later shells would start exploding nearby.

My father and Mek eventually joined my mother in Subotica. When she sufficiently recovered from her gall-bladder surgery, my parents moved to Novi Sad, not far away from Subotica, where Mama's other brother owned a little one-bedroom apartment. They spent a year or so there, trying all along to get the papers to emigrate to Canada. During that time, Tata was often gone for weeks, working in Hungary with Dragan's construction company. Mama longed for Sarajevo, was devastated with what was happening in Bosnia, insulted by the relentless Serbian propaganda that was pouring out of TV and radio. She spent days crying, and Mek would put his head in her lap and look up at her with his moist setter look, and my mother talked to him as to her only friend. Every day, she had a hard time confronting the fact that they had lost everything they'd worked for their whole life; the only remnant of their comfortable previous life was the gorgeous Irish setter.

The one-bedroom in Novi Sad was often full of refugees from Bosnia – friends of friends or family of the family – whom my parents put up until the unfortunate people could make it to Germany or France or some other place where they were not wanted and never would be. They slept scattered all over the floor, my mother stepping over the bodies on her way to the bathroom, Mek always at her heels. He never bothered the refugees, never barked at those miserable people. He let the children pet him.

Young male that he was, Mek would often brawl with other dogs. Once, when my mother took him out, he got into a confrontation with a mean Rottweiler. She tried to separate them, unwisely, as they were about to go at each other's throats, and the Rottweiler tore my mother's hand apart. My sister Tina was there at the time, and she took Mama to the emergency room where they had absolutely nothing needed to treat the injury; they did give her the address of a doctor who could sell them the bandages and a tetanus shot. They spent all of the money they had to pay the doctor and then take a cab back home. In fact, they didn't have enough to pay the cab and the driver said he'd come the next day to get the rest of the money. My sister bluntly told him that there was no reason for him to come back, for they'd have no money tomorrow, or the day after tomorrow, or any time soon. (The cabbie didn't insist: the daily inflation in Serbia at that time was about 300 per cent, and the money would have been worthless by the next day anyway.) For years afterwards, Mama could not move her hand properly or grip anything with it. Mek would go crazy if he but smelled a Rottweiler on the same block.

In the fall of 1993, my parents and sister finally got all the papers and the plane tickets for Canada. Family and friends came over to bid them farewell. Everyone was sure they'd never see them again, and my parents and sister knew that emigrating to Canada would irreversibly sever all connections with their previous life. There were a lot of tears, as at a funeral. Mek figured out that something was up; he never let my mother or father out of his sight, as if worried they might leave him; he became especially cuddly, putting his head into their laps whenever he could, leaning against their shins when lying down. Touched though my father may have been with Mek's love, he didn't want to take him along to Canada – he couldn't know what was waiting for them there; where they'd live, whether they'd be able to take care of themselves, let alone a dog. Tata called me in Chicago to demand from me that I reason with Mama and Tina and convince them that Mek must be left behind. 'Mek is family,' I told him. 'Do not cross the ocean without him.' But I knew that Tata had a point and my heart sunk to my stomach at the thought of their leaving him. My mother could not bring herself to discuss the possibility of moving to Canada without him; she just wept at the very thought of abandoning him with people who were strangers to him.

Back in Sarajevo, my friend Veba had gotten married and moved out of the apartment across the street from us. Don had to stay with Veba's mother and brother because Veba's duties kept him away from home for long stretches, while his wife, who worked for the Red Cross, was also often gone. Following a Red Cross official on an inspection of a Bosnian POW camp, Veba's wife discovered that her father-in-law was alive. Ever since Veba's father had failed to return home from work at the beginning of war, Don would leap – prompted by the question, 'Where is Vlado?' – at the coat rack where Veba's father used to hang up his uniform. Although čika-Vlado would be released from the POW camp toward the end of the war, Don would never see him again.

I received only intermittent news from Veba's family – Veba's letter mailed by a foreign friend who could go in and out of the Bosnian war zone; a sudden, late-night call from a satellite phone, arranged by a friend who worked for a foreign journalists' pool. During the siege the regular phone lines were most often down, but every once in a while they would inexplicably work, so I'd randomly try to reach

Veba. One late night in 1994, I called Veba's family from Chicago on a whim. It was very early morning in Sarajevo, but Veba's mother picked up the phone after one ring. She was sobbing, so my first thought was that Veba was dead. She composed herself enough to tell me that he was fine, but that someone had poisoned their dog. Don had been in horrible pain all night, retching and vomiting yellow slime, she said; he'd died just a moment before I called. Veba was there too; upon hearing the news, he'd biked from his new place in the middle of the night, the curfew still on, risking his life. He'd made it in time to hold Don as he expired, and was crying on the phone with me. I could find no words for him, as I could never provide any consolation for any of my friends under siege. Veba wrapped Don in a blanket, carried him down the fifteen flights of stairs and buried him with his favourite tennis ball in the long-abandoned construction site behind the high-rise.

My father finally surrendered. In December 1993, my parents, sister and Mek drove to Budapest. At the airport, my sister negotiated a cheap ticket and a place in the cargo hold for Mek. After they arrived in Canada, I rushed over from Chicago to see them for the first time in two very rough years. As soon as I walked in the door of their barely furnished fifteenth-floor apartment in Hamilton, Ontario, Mek ran toward me, wagging his tail. I was astonished that he remembered me after nearly two years. I'd felt that large parts of my Sarajevo self had vanished, but when Mek put his head in my lap, some of me came back.

Mek had a happy life in Hamilton. My mother always said that he was a 'lucky boy'. He died in 2007, at the age of seventeen. My parents would never consider having a dog again. My mother confides in a parakeet these days, and cries whenever Mek is but mentioned.

Veba moved to Canada in 1998. He lives in Montreal with his wife and children. He's never had a dog after Don. My sister lives in London. She has not had a dog since Mek. I married a woman who has never lived without a dog and now have a Rhodesian ridgeback named Billie. ■

CONTRIBUTORS

Daniel Alarcón's *Lost City Radio* won the International Literature Award in 2009. He is founder of Radio Ambulante, a Spanish-language storytelling podcast.

John Barth is Professor Emeritus in the Johns Hopkins Writing Seminars. He is a recipient of the National Book Award, the F. Scott Fitzgerald Award and the PEN/Malamud Award. His essay collection, *Final Fridays*, is published by Counterpoint Press in 2012.

Ann Beattie's books include the story collections *What Was Mine* and *Follies*, the novel *Chilly Scenes of Winter* and the novella *Walks With Men*. She is the author of *Mrs. Nixon*, forthcoming from Scribner, and recipient of the PEN/Malamud Award.

Sophie Cabot Black's collections include *The Misunderstanding of Nature* and *The Descent*. She received the Grolier Poetry Prize and the Poetry Society of America's John Masefield Memorial Award.

Paula Bohince is the author of two poetry collections, *Incident at the Edge of Bayonet Woods* and *The Children*, which is forthcoming from Sarabande Books.

Judy Chicurel's writing has appeared in the *New York Times*, *Newsday* and *Parenting*. Her plays have been performed at the New York International Fringe Festival and Sage Theater. She is a 2011 fellow at the Writers' Institute at the City University of New York Graduate Center.

Aleksandar Hemon was born in Sarajevo in 1964 and has lived in Chicago since 1992. He is the author of the novel *The Lazarus Project* and three collections of short stories: *The Question of Bruno*; *Nowhere Man*; and *Love and Obstacles*.

Ishion Hutchinson was born in Port Antonio, Jamaica. His first collection, *Far District*, won the PEN/Joyce Osterweil Award.

Stacy Kranitz is the recipient of a Young Photographers' Alliance Award. Her photographs have been published in *Elle*, *Fortune*, *Metropolis*, *Mother Jones*, the *New York Times*, *Rolling Stone*, *Vice* and *Wired*, among other publications.

David Long's books include the short-story collection *Blue Spruce* and the novels *The Falling Boy*, *The Daughters of Simon Lamoreaux* and *The Inhabited World*.

Vanessa Manko was formerly Dance Editor of the *Brooklyn Rail*. She has danced with the Charleston Ballet Theater and taught writing at SUNY Purchase and New York University. 'The Interrogation' is an extract from her first novel, *The Un-American*.

Claire Messud's *The Emperor's Children* was longlisted for the 2006 Man Booker Prize. Her next novel, *The Woman Upstairs*, is published in 2013 by Virago Press.

Susan Minot is the author of the novels *Monkeys, Folly, Evening* and *Rapture*, and the story collections *Lust and Other Stories* and *Poems 4 A.M.* 'Thirty Girls' is based on the real story of the Lord's Resistance Army kidnapping of Catholic schoolgirls in northern Uganda.

Alice Munro's stories have appeared in numerous publications including the *New Yorker*, the *Atlantic* and the *Paris Review*. Her recent collections include *The View from Castle Rock* and *Too Much Happiness*. She is a three-time winner of Canada's Governor General's Award. In 2009, she was awarded the Man Booker International Prize for her lifetime body of work.

Jacob Newberry is pursuing a PhD in Creative Writing (Poetry) at Florida State University. His poetry and non-fiction have appeared in the *Iowa Review*, *Crab Orchard Review* and *Best New Poets 2011*, among others. He is currently in Jerusalem on a Fulbright Fellowship in Creative Writing.

Chinelo Okparanta was born in Port Harcourt, Nigeria. She received her BS from Pennsylvania State University, her MA from Rutgers University and her MFA from the Iowa Writers' Workshop. She teaches at the University of Iowa.

Adrienne Rich is the recipient of a Lannan Lifetime Achievement Award, the National Book Award, a MacArthur Fellowship and a 2010 Griffin Poetry Prize Lifetime Recognition Award. Her most recent collection is *Tonight No Poetry Will Serve: Poems 2007–2010*.

Anne Tyler is the author of eighteen books. Her novel *The Accidental Tourist* won the National Book Critics Circle Award in 1988. In 1989 she won the Pulitzer Prize for her novel *Breathing Lessons*. 'The Beginner's Goodbye' is an extract from her novel of the same name, published in April 2012 by Knopf in the US and Chatto & Windus in the UK.

GRANTA 118: WINTER 2012 | EVENTS

Granta's events are free and open to the public unless otherwise stated. RSVP to events@granta.com.

LONDON

Exit Strategies Live
7 February, time and venue tbc
In this special edition of Liars' League, actors from the live fiction salon perform stories from *Granta*'s latest issue.

The London Launch
9 February, 6.30 p.m., Foyles, 113–119 Charing Cross Road, London WC2H 0EB
Granta contributors and editors launch the new issue with drinks and conversation.

NEW YORK

The New York Launch
7 February, 7 p.m., BookCourt, 163 Court Street, Brooklyn, NY 11201
An evening of reading, drinks and conversation with *Granta* 118 contributors Judy Chicurel, Vanessa Manko and Susan Minot.

Thirty Girls, The Interrogation and City Boy
9 February, 7 p.m., 192 BOOKS, 192 10th Avenue, New York, NY 10011
Join *Granta* 118 contributors Judy Chicurel, Vanessa Manko and Susan Minot to launch the new issue.

The Way Out
13 February, 7 p.m., McNally Jackson, 52 Prince Street, New York, NY 10012
Join Exit Strategies poets Sophie Cabot Black, Paula Bohince, Ishion Hutchinson and Rowan Ricardo Phillips for readings that explore fleeing one's life, phantoms and choice.

TEL AVIV

The Tel Aviv Launch
9 February, 7 p.m., Sipur Pashut, 36 Shabazi Street, Neve Tezedek, Tel Aviv 65150
Join contributor Jacob Newberry and guests to explore personal and political exit strategies.

GRANTA ACROSS AMERICA

SEATTLE, WA
7 February, 7 p.m., Elliott Bay Book Company, 1521 10th Avenue, Seattle, WA 98122
David Long reads from and discusses 'Bonfire', his story of lust and nostalgia.

MIAMI, FL
7 February, 7 p.m., Books & Books, 265 Aragon Avenue, Coral Gables, FL 33134
John Barth reads and discusses his essay 'The End?', muse-inviting rituals and writing 'nothing'.

BOSTON, MA
9 February, 7 p.m., Harvard Book Store, 1256 Massachusetts Avenue, Cambridge, MA 02138
Claire Messud discusses her essay 'The Road to Damascus', memory, loss and the search for the Beirut of her father's childhood.

IOWA CITY, IA
9 February, 7 p.m., Prairie Lights, 15 South Dubuque Street, Iowa City, IA 52240
Join Chinelo Okparanta for a reading of her *Granta* story 'America'.

SAN FRANCISCO, CA
9 February, 6.30 p.m., City Lights, 261 Columbus Avenue, San Francisco, CA 94133
Join Daniel Alarcón and other *Granta* writers for a literary evening celebrating the launch of Exit Strategies.

CHICAGO, IL
10 February, 7.30 p.m., Women & Children First, 5233 North Clark Street, Chicago, IL 60640
Granta's New Voice Chinelo Okparanta joins local *Granta* authors for readings of their work.

LITERARY FESTIVALS

Granta will also be participating in the following international literary festivals. Please check granta.com or the festival websites for details.

GALLE FORT, SRI LANKA
Galle Literary Festival
18 – 22 January
www.galleliteraryfestival.com

Exit Strategies Launch
19 January:
Susan Minot in conversation with Ellah Allfrey.

Writing Political Realities into Fiction
20 January:
A panel discussion with Ellah Allfrey, Romesh Gunesekera, Hari Kunzru and Susan Minot.

IOWA CITY, USA
Mission Creek Festival
27 March – 1 April
www.festival.missionfreak.com